WHY PLAY POKER?

1. It's incredibly entertaining.
2. Why should the boys have all the fun?
3. Speaking of men, it's a great way to meet them.
4. And men think girls who play cards are daring and sexy.
5. Whether or not you fill your little black book with numbers, you can fill your wallet with your winnings.
6. Over 100 million players + 2.5 million possible hands + 100s of kinds of poker = 1 million possibilities for different games and gatherings.
7. Doesn't matter if a guy is bigger or stronger, poker's won by brains and heart.
8. You can learn things from playing poker that can improve your love life.
9. You'll get to know your friends better—and be able to tell when they're lying.
10. It's through the risks you take that you learn the most about yourself, and just what kind of a badass you are.

THE BADASS GIRL'S GUIDE TO POKER

ALL YOU NEED
TO BEAT THE BOYS

TOBY LEAH BOCHAN

Adams Media
Avon, Massachusetts

Published by Adams Media,
an F+W Publications Company
57 Littlefield Street, Avon, MA 02322. U.S.A.
www.adamsmedia.com

ISBN: 1-59337-397-X

Printed in Canada.

J I H G F E D C B

Library of Congress Cataloging-in-Publication Data
Bochan, Toby Leah.
The badass girl's guide to poker / Toby Leah Bochan.
p.   cm.
ISBN 1-59337-397-X
1. Poker for women. 2. Poker—Social aspects. I. Title.
GV1252.W66B63 2005
795.412—dc22
                    2004030418

This publication is designed to provide accurate and authoritative information
with regard to the subject matter covered. It is sold with the understanding that
the publisher is not engaged in rendering legal, accounting, or other professional advice. If legal advice or other expert assistance is required, the services
of a competent professional person should be sought.

—From a *Declaration of Principles* jointly adopted by a
Committee of the American Bar Association and a
Committee of Publishers and Associations

Many of the designations used by manufacturers and sellers to distinguish their
product are claimed as trademarks. Where those designations appear in this
book and Adams Media was aware of a trademark claim, the designations have
been printed with initial capital letters.

This book is available at quantity discounts for bulk purchases.
For information, please call 1-800-872-5627.

For my parents, Karen Laurie Roston and Peter Bochan, for staking me in my first game and supporting me through every crazy gamble I've taken in life with enthusiasm and love.

CONTENTS

INTRODUCTION

CARDS IN THE AIR

It's the game the boys like best
Two or three times a week
One man often beats the rest
With nothing else but cheek.
— G. W. ALLEN, *POKER RULES IN RHYME*

O ne day when I was five or six years old, my father picked up a deck of cards and asked me if I wanted to learn to play a new game. I loved to play cards, and always ate up new games as quickly as they were served up to me, from go fish to war to solitaire to crazy 8s to gin. I loved the physical act of holding a hand of cards: how you could make a fan of them, choose to match up the suits, or put the numbers in order. And unlike when we played Scrabble on board game night, I could win at cards.

A new game? Without a pause, I agreed, and asked, "How do you play?" To answer, he tossed the entire deck in the air. The game: fifty-two-card pickup. I stood, agape as the cards fluttered down all over our living room. "Pick 'em up!" my father said, laughing, at which point I burst into tears.

Yeah, I got upset over that whole "got your nose" trick when I was younger, too. I was perhaps a little too serious as a kid.

I was seven the first time I played poker. It was summer—my parents and I were visiting with family friends in a house out of the city, and for some reason, my first-grade teacher had been invited as well. I went to an extremely progressive elementary school in Manhattan, so this didn't phase me. And Steve, as I called my teacher, played cards with me all the time in class.

I loved playing cards. Maybe one reason is that I was a very competitive child. I was so convinced I had achieved the highest score ever playing Missile Command on my Atari 2600 that I made my dad take a Polaroid to send in. Where exactly he was supposed to send it in, I'm not sure. At that time, with math being my favorite subject, I dreamed of, no joke, being a supermarket cashier when I grew up. What can I say? I loved to make change.

So naturally, I loved the chips. We had a set of plastic chips in red, white, and blue that I had spent lazy afternoons building imaginary cities with, patriotic round buildings populating the streets. The chips were grooved so the stacks would hold steady until a "disaster" struck and I would send the buildings clattering down with a mighty swipe, enjoying the sound of the chips clattering against one another.

My parents played poker semiregularly with friends for a while, but it was usually after I was sent to bed, and I suppose some of their guests might have thought having a kid in the game would be a killjoy. But this summer afternoon, there was no excuse: I had already learned the basics of five-card draw and seven-card stud and I figured my first-grade teacher was as much my friend as theirs. We had played cards together already!

I knew about money, but since I had none of my own, a nickel wasn't any more meaningful to me than a white chip. They were just pieces used to play the game, just like the plastic houses and play money in Monopoly. They gave me three stacks of chips and I built my cities, dreaming of expansion.

As the afternoon progressed, I learned new games with exotic names like "anaconda" and "black Mariah," and by the time the game finished, I had more than doubled my chips (well, by one). I pushed my towers toward my father and received $2.51—a veritable fortune in candy and comic books. I was hooked.

I played as much as I could in my parents' game and any others I could find, but I didn't start playing poker regularly until I moved to Texas, home of cowboys, barbecue, and poker legends. I was in graduate school there, and after a failed attempt to bring a bunch of writers together every week to play basketball, someone had the more appealing idea (to a bunch of sedentary smokers and drinkers) to start a weekly poker game. We played dealer's choice, and the nights were full of beer and wildcards. Most of the games we played involved a great deal of luck, and I don't remember if I won or lost most of the time—I was there purely to enjoy the game and the company, and to have fun.

It was years after I moved back to New York City that I truly got bitten by the poker bug. Two things happened: My best friend got engaged to a man, Greg, who played poker regularly, and my own engagement went sour. It was at their wedding in August 2003 when I first sat down with the guys who would become my regular poker buddies. Drunk by this time, I protested that I had only watched Texas hold'em on TV and was in no state to learn to play for real, but two of the guys staked me (paid for my chips) and a third promised to explain the fine points as the game went on. My then fiancé, no risk-taker, watched for a while and then went back to our room. I didn't notice. I was immediately caught up in the action—though terribly confused about bets called "blinds" and what was worth playing. I hadn't had such fun in months.

When I finally got the tits to leave my fiancé, I knew one of my coping mechanisms would be to keep busy, and one of the first things I got involved in was poker. I begged Greg to invite me anytime there was a seat free in his regular game, and I devoured books on strategy. I organized trips to casinos and card rooms and found out about underground tournaments. And the more I played, the more I saw how popular poker had become—and how many people around me also played.

Gone is the image of poker as a game of degenerates and cheats, long games played in the backrooms of bordellos—no longer will people wonder if you have a "gambling problem" if you spend a night a week with your poker pals, or take a weekend trip just to play in a casino. The stigma has turned to status. Now, knowing poker impresses people—it gives you an image as a smart risk-taker, a trendsetter, a chick who's no chicken, a woman not easily intimidated—it makes you a badass.

I hope you enjoy this book even a quarter as much as I enjoy playing poker, and fall in love with the game as I did, because I'd really like to meet more badass babes across the felt from me.

—Toby Leah Bochan

SECTION ONE

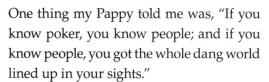

ANTE UP

One thing my Pappy told me was, "If you know poker, you know people; and if you know people, you got the whole dang world lined up in your sights."

There's enough sense in that to make the game worth all the trouble it can get you into.

—BRET MAVERICK

1

HOLDING YOUR OWN HAND: POKER 101

*Remember, Ginger Rogers did everything Fred Astaire did,
but she did it backwards and in high heels.*

—FAITH WHITTLESEY

oker's one of those games they say things about like "It takes only a few minutes to learn, but a lifetime to master." If your only exposure to poker is from seeing it onscreen, it may seem like a complicated, intimidating game. But it's not: if you can learn the rules to Clue or Boggle, you can learn to play poker.

READING THE CARDS

The first step toward your femme fatale future in poker is to understand the cards.

Open a deck of cards and you'll find fifty-two black and red cards in four suits, each suit containing thirteen cards. Going from lowest to highest, the cards are: 2-3-4-5-6-7-8-9-10-jack-queen-king-ace. The ace can stand for 1 or 11, making it both the lowest and highest card in the deck, the alpha and omega. It makes the ace a very sneaky and powerful card. There's a reason why an ace in the hole is a good thing.

When talking about the cards, people will use the word *rank* to describe them. It can mean two things:

1. It's a fancy way of saying what number it stands for. If you hear someone say he's got two cards of the same "rank" it means he's got two of a kind, such as two 3s or two queens.
2. If someone says she's got a card of a "higher rank" than yours, it means it beats your card. It's pretty self-explanatory: a 3 will beat a 2, a 10 beats 9 through 2, kings win against queens and lower, and so on.

Technically, the suits themselves are ranked, though the fact of the matter is it hardly ever matters. Still, it's good to know: (from highest to lowest) spades, hearts, diamonds, clubs. A good trick to remembering this is that the ranking of suits goes in reverse alphabetical order.

What is more important to understand about suits is that you'll often hear people talking about cards being "suited" or "unsuited." If two or more cards in your hand are the same suit—say, two hearts—they're said to be "suited." Cards that are of different suits are "unsuited." They're also referred to as "off-suit."

Now let's look at what we do with the cards.

RANKING THE HANDS

The first thing you've gotta learn is what beats what. What wins. You've got to learn that flushes beat straights just as intuitively as you know that rock beats scissors, scissors cuts paper, paper covers rock.

In most games of poker, the winner is determined by who can make the best five-card hand. There are games like draw where you only get five cards, but there are others like seven-card stud or Texas hold'em, where you pick the best five from seven cards. I'll explain more in the next chapter. What's important to understand at this point is that poker's about the best five cards. Think of it as the Jackson Five or the Fab Five if it helps you remember.

From a fifty-two-card deck, there are over 2½ million possible combinations of five-card hands (2,598,960 to be precise). The harder (or more unlikely, odds-wise) it is to get the hand, the higher it's ranked.

A note on notations:

When talking about the cards in a hand, I'll shorten aces, kings, queens, and jacks to their initial: A, K, Q, J, respectively. Look, on the cards themselves it doesn't say "king," just "K," so you've got to get used it.

Going from the absolute best hand to the lowest:

2 ♥ 3 ♥ 4 ♥ 5 ♥ 6 ♥ (Straight Flush)

Five cards, of the same suit, in order. The 2-3-4-5-6 of hearts is a 6-high straight flush, since the highest card is a 6. The only thing that can beat it is a higher straight flush, such as the 7-8-9-10-J of clubs. The highest straight flush is 10-J-Q-K-A, which is called a *royal flush*. Nothing beats a royal flush.

10 ♠ 10 ♥ 10 ♦ 10 ♣ 5 ♠ (Four of a Kind)

Four of the same card, such as 8-8-8-8. It doesn't matter what the fifth card is in this hand. No one will give that 5 a second glance—they'll be focused on the glorious wonder of your four 10s.

9 ♠ 9 ♥ 9 ♣ 7 ♥ 7 ♦ (Full House)

Three of a kind plus a pair, such as 9-9-9-7-7. If two full houses are up against each other, the one with the higher three of a kind wins. Example: Q-Q-Q-2-2 totally whips the tar out of J-J-J-K-K. It doesn't matter that kings are a higher rank than queens. The three queens are up against the three silly jacks, and they win. The kings? As irrelevant as remembering the name of your high school prom king.

2 ♣ 7 ♣ 8 ♣ 10 ♣ K ♣ (Flush)

If your cards are smartly dressed, all in the same suit, but a little out of order, you've got a flush. A flush is any five cards of the same suit, but not in a row. So 6-8-10-J-A all of diamonds is a flush. If two flushes are competing for the high hand, the flush with the highest card wins. So, a diamond flush with an ace would beat a club flush with a king as the highest card, for example.

8 ♦ 9 ♥ 10 ♣ J ♠ Q ♦ (Straight)

Five cards in numerical order, but not of the same suit. If you had a 5 of clubs, 6 of diamonds, 7 of spades, 8 of clubs, and a 9 of hearts, you'd call it a straight "to the 9."

J ♣ J ♦ J ♠ 7 ♦ 3 ♠ (Three of a Kind)
Three of the same card, like 4-4-4. Three's good company.

6 ♠ 6 ♣ 2 ♦ 2 ♠ A ♥ (Two Pair)
Isn't that cute? You've got two 2s and two 6s hanging out together—it's kind of like a double date. If two pair is up against another two pair, the highest pair of them all wins it. Kings and 3s beats queens and 10s, and so on. The second pair only matters if both players' high pair is the same: K-K-9-9 would beat K-K-3-3. In the unlikely event that both players have exactly the same two pair, that last card, called "a kicker," can decide it. For example, K-K-3-3-A would beat K-K-3-3-9.

8 ♣ 8 ♦ J ♠ 5 ♥ 2 ♣ (Pair)
Sometimes a couple just wants privacy. If you've got two cards that are the same, say two 10s, in your hand, you've got a pair. Higher-ranked pairs beat lower pairs, and if two players have the same pair, the player with the higher kicker wins: 10-10-K-7-2 beats 10-10-J-9-4.

A ♥ Q ♦ 10 ♠ 7 ♠ 4 ♣ (High Card)
One is the loneliest number. If there's no pair, no nothing, just a jumbled mess of numbers and suits, players pit their highest card against one another. Just hope yours is an ace.

⭐A Few Badass Tricks to Help Keep It Straight

It's all about what's harder to get. It's easy to see that two pair will beat just one, but when it gets to straights, flushes, and full houses, people often become confused. After all, you have to have all five cards just right to make any of those three hands, so why is one better than the others? Getting five cards in a row seems harder than just a bunch of the same suit.

I personally find it easiest to remember by figuring out how many cards in the deck can make that hand. Look at it this way:

- To make a full house, you only have eight cards to work with, because you need a set of three and a pair. They've got to be of the same rank, so you've only got four cards available to make that three of a kind, and four to get that pair. Just eight measly cards.
- To make a flush, your five cards can be composed of any cards of the same suit in the deck. That's thirteen cards.
- To make a straight, while rank matters, suit doesn't. So while you need five cards in a row, each one can be any suit. So you've got four cards that will work for each of five spots, or twenty cards.

I said before that there are 2,598,960 possible five-card combinations in a fifty-two-card deck. If you're a numbers nut, it may help to look at how many of those combinations exist for each hand.

Hand	Number of Combinations
Straight Flush	40
Four of a Kind	624
Full House	3,744
Flush	5,108
Straight	10,200
Three of a Kind	54,912
Two Pair	123,552
One Pair	1,098,240
High Card	1,302,540
Total	2,598,960

On the other hand, if numbers just make your head hurt, just make up a mnemonic device that works for you, such as "A house full of monkeys is a harder to deal with than a toilet that won't flush, I'll tell you straight." Works for me on so many levels.

ON THE OTHER END: THE LOWEST HAND

In some games of poker, the lowest hand wins, or the pot is split between the highest and lowest hands.

The lowest hand is usually defined as A-2-3-4-5 of any suit—even the same suit. Aces are low. In some home games, the "low" hand is defined instead as the "worst" hand. The worst possible five-card hand in poker would be A-2-3-4-6 unsuited. Whatever the case, the lowest hand should be defined before you start playing for the night.

If, at the end of a low hand, you're confused and can't decide which one is lowest, there's an easy way to figure it out. Here's the trick: Look at the hands and decide which one would beat which if you were playing that the high hand wins the pot. The hand that would sit at the bottom of the pile, the biggest loser? That's the low-hand winner. Think of it as bizarro poker.

Example: A-2-3-5-7 would ordinarily lose to A-2-3-5-8, so it's the lower hand and wins.

Now see if you can figure it out—who wins?

Player 1: A-2-4-7-8
Player 2: A-4-5-6-8
Player 3: 2-3-4-5-7

If you picked Player 3, give yourself a prize. The other two hands are "higher" hands because they have an 8 high. It doesn't matter that they both contain a lower card than 2—it's the 8 that kills them.

If it were just between Player 1 and 2, Player 2 would win—the hands would be judged on the second-highest card. If the second-highest card tied, you'd check the third-highest card and so on and so on and Scooby dooby do, yeah! Sorry, bizarro poker makes me think of bizarre song associations. Moving on.

MONEY MAKES THE GAME GO AROUND

Most people think that poker is a game of cards, and it is, but what separates it out from bridge or crazy 8s or hearts is that it's a game played for money. Even in strip poker you're playing for the currency of clothes—though, of course, your objective in that game may not be to win, exactly. Money is the way score is kept in the game of poker—a player who's got more money, chips, or even M&Ms than she started with is winning at the game.

Most of the time, it's chips. Instead of throwing actual dollars and coins on the table, players use chips that stand for different amounts of money. What amount chips stand for depends on the *stakes* of the game—how much you're playing for. The magic of chips is that the same chips can stand for penny-nickel-dime one day and $10-$20-$40 the next. They also make the betting simpler, which keeps the game flowing.

Before you start playing, you'll trade your real cash dollars for plastic or clay chips and "buy in" to the game. There may be a minimum or set buy-in for the game you're playing. Otherwise, decide the amount you "buy in" for by the stakes—say ten to twenty times the amount of the biggest bet possible. Err on the side of excess—it puts you in a better frame of mind to sit down at the table and feel like you're positively *dripping* with chips than to sit with a skimpy stack and feel like you're way underdressed for the occasion. Or just pick a cute player and ask what he started with.

⋆Badass Betting Basics

Before a hand is even dealt, players put money in the pot. This way, each player has something at stake in the game even before she knows what she'll be betting on.

There are two different ways this is done.

Antes

You've heard the phrase "ante up" in other contexts, meaning "pay up." It originates from poker. Generally, if a game has an ante, every player contributes a predetermined amount to the pot before each hand. It's usually set the same as the minimum amount anyone can bet, so in a nickel-dime-quarter game, it would be a nickel. In some home games, players take turns dealing and the ante rotates around with the deal, to speed things up. No matter if the dealer puts the whole kit and kaboodle into the pot or if everyone antes up, it doesn't count as a bet from anyone. It's just there to sweeten the kitty.

Blinds

The other way to start the action rolling is by making players put in a forced bet, called a "blind," before the deal. The most common practice is to have the two players to the left of the dealer pay the blinds. The player immediately to the dealer's left places a smaller bet called the "little blind," while the player two places to the left puts in the "big blind."

The amounts of the blinds are fixed and determined before the game begins. Usually the "big blind" is equal to the smallest bet possible, while the little blind is ½ or ⅓ of that amount. So, if the minimum bet was $3, the big blind would place a forced bet of $3 and the little blind might put out $1.

The difference between blinds and antes is that blinds *do* count as a player's first bet. This means in the first round of betting, no one can "check," that is, everyone has to bet to stay in the hand. *Checking out other players* is always optional, but if there are blind bets, you have to put in at least the amount of the big blind to stay in the hand.

☆How a Round of Betting Goes

You're the first to act in a game with antes. There are two things you can do: *check* (decide not to bet, or pass) or you can *bet*. Let's say you bet.

The next player (the one sitting on your left) can do three things: She can *call*, or *see* your bet, which means she matches it exactly (if you bet $3, she would call $3); she can *raise* the bet (she matches your $3 and then adds another $3 to it, making it $6 for the next player to call); or she can give up on her hand and *fold* it.

This continues from player to player going around to the left. If someone raises a bet you made, when it comes back to you, you have the same options as everyone else: call, raise, or fold. The round of betting is over when everyone simply calls the last bet and all the players (who haven't folded) have put in the same amount of money. A round of betting can also be "checked around"—meaning everyone checks and there's no money put in the pot that round.

One way to indicate that you're checking is to tap your fingers on the table. So there's a perfectly good reason why you *need* to paint those pretty nails before the game. You don't want something as superficial as chipped polish to chip away at your confidence.

Now, how do you know how much you can bet when it's your turn? That depends on what kind of game you're playing in. Shall we?

BASIC BETTING

There's no one rule of how to set up the betting in all games of poker. Depending on whether you're playing in a casino or in a home game, you may encounter one of these four common structures. In home games, they may be much looser with the rules, so be sure to ask for details. It is your money, after all, and you should know how to use it so you don't lose it.

✴Spread Limit

Home games are often spread-limit games. What this means is that a player can bet or raise any amount within some range—for instance $1 to $5. Basically, it means the minimum any player can bet is $1, and the most anyone can bet or raise at one time is $5. The only other rule deals with raising. If someone raises, you can only raise that much or higher. In other words, if the schmuck to your left raises $3, you can't raise just the $2 you were planning to; you've got to raise $3, or more, or call. If you sit down at a home game and some guy hands you two stacks of chips and tells you, "White's a dollar, red's two, max raise five bucks," you're playing in a $1 to $5 spread-limit game.

✴Fixed Limit

This is what most people play in casinos. Simply, with fixed-limit poker, the amount you can bet or raise is fixed for each round of betting. If you're playing a $2 to $4 fixed-limit game, every player can *only* bet or raise $2 for the first few rounds (usually the first two) of betting, and can *only* bet or raise $4 for the last rounds of betting. It keeps it nice and simple. You drop the word "fixed" when talking about this kind of betting—just say, "I was playing 3–6 limit hold'em." Or, to be even more badass, drop "limit," too, and simply declare, "I played 4–8 hold'em all night!"

☆Pot Limit

In pot-limit games, you can bet or raise any amount up to the total amount that's in the pot right then. So if the pot has $30 in it at that very moment, you could bet anything from a buck to the whole $30. It seems pretty simple, but it actually gets kind of complicated—and can be very expensive if people keep doubling the pot by raising everything they can.

☆No Limit

If you've watched Texas hold'em on television, you've seen the world of no limit. It's just what it sounds like: at any point, you can push in all the chips you have in front of you as a bet. There's absolutely no cap on how much money that is, other than it's what you have on the table already.

Understand what wins? Check. Know how the money works? Check.

Now you're ready to sit down at a table and learn how the games are played.

KNOW HOW TO HOLD'EM: POPULAR POKER GAMES

There are few things that are so unpardonably neglected in our country as poker. Why, I have known clergymen, good men, kind-hearted, liberal, sincere, and all that, who did not know the meaning of a "flush." It is enough to make one ashamed of the species.

—MARK TWAIN

orry, I'm not going to start by teaching you the rules of Texas hold'em. I've misled you, but for a purpose. Misdirection and deception are part of every game of poker, and there is a lot more to poker than the much-televised game of Texas hold'em.

Back in the old days—by which I mean just over thirty years ago—the champion of the World Series of Poker was the best all-around player, not just the person who could play one game the best. The first World Series, in fact, wasn't even a showdown tournament, where the player who ended up with all the chips took the title. Instead, all the players decided who the best player in the world was. (Poker legend Johnny Moss received the honor.) And while it may seem like Texas hold'em is the only game in town during the WSOP, in 2004, there were thirty-three events in a wide variety of poker games. The fact of the matter is that if you're going to join any home game, they'll probably play a variety of games. You need to stock your card closet with all the essentials you might need to pull out during an evening of poker.

Only knowing hold'em is like going to a dance and only knowing the twist. If you're a ballroom dancer and you only know the waltz, you're not going to get very far. Okay, you may even become a world-class waltzer, Matilda, but how embarrassing would it be for a champion waltzer to be asked to Fox Trot and have to say, "Er . . . sorry, not familiar with that one." My point is, there aren't waltzers, there are ballroom dancers, and there aren't hold'em-ers, there are poker players.

So I don't repeat myself, here are rules for all the games:

- If you're the dealer, deal the cards one at a time in a round starting with the player to your left—clockwise.
- Betting also moves around the table clockwise.
- If people have folded, don't deal to them anymore. They're out of the game.
- When all the cards are dealt and the betting is done, the players who are left in the hand show their cards. It's called the "showdown," and the player who initiated the last bet of the hand is the first to show her cards.

Now let's get started.

FIVE-CARD DRAW

Picture it:

Five cowboys sit around an old wooden table in a saloon, cigarettes hanging from their lips, a pile of coins and old dollars in the center of the table, surrounded by mugs of beer and dirty glasses of whiskey. They look at the five cards in their hands and consider what to do as a player piano provides the soundtrack. One sinister-looking mustachioed fellow hands in two cards and gets two in return from the dealer. The next changes three, and the next two switch just a single card. The betting begins, and it continues until only two players remain—Mr. Mustache and a desperate farm owner. Raise follows raise until the deed to the farm tops the watches and gold as the final bet. The saloon gets quiet with anticipation as the two men lay out their hands on the table for all to see. Can farm boy beat four kings and save the farm?

This is poker at it's most traditional—it's five-card draw. It's the poker of movies, of *Maverick* and John Wayne Westerns.

Even though it's fallen out of favor and is never really played in casinos, five-card draw is still an important game to learn. It's the basic black dress of your poker wardrobe. If you play in a home game and somehow you don't know the rules—well, it'll just look bad. You won't be thought of as much of a card player to say the least, and that's the least that will be said about you once you leave the table. The other good thing about knowing five-card draw is that it's a relatively quick and easy game to learn, so it's a good place to start.

⋆ How to Play Five-Card Draw
Maximum number of players: 6–7

1. All players ante up.
2. The dealer deals each player five cards, face down.
3. All the players pick up their cards from the table and check out what they've got.
4. There's a round of betting, starting with the player to the dealer's left.
5. When the betting is done, those who are still in the hand get to trade in one, two, or three cards from their hand for new ones. If a player has an ace, she can trade in the other four cards in her hand, but she has to show her ace.

   Note: *You don't have to trade any cards—if you've already got a straight or better, you'll want to "stand pat" and keep the cards you were first dealt.*
6. After all the players receive their new cards, there's another round of betting, starting with the first player who is still in the hand to the dealer's left.
7. After the betting is completed, players show their hands and the best one takes the pot.

⋆ Basic Strategy
Considering your cards

So you've got five cards. Now you have to decide whether they're any good and what to do with them. Obviously, if you're dealt four aces, you know you've got a good hand, but the chances of that happening are astronomical.

The majority of hands that you're first dealt in five-card draw will have a pair or just a high card. Same's true for everyone at the table, and a high pair is often the winning hand.

Say your hand is: 4 ♦ 4 ♥ 5 ♦ 6 ♥ K ♥

What's a girl to do?

1. You could trade your 4 and 5 of diamonds and hope to get two more hearts to match your 4, 6, and king

2. You could trade in one 4 and the king and hope to make a straight.

3. You could trade in everything but the 4s and hope for three of a kind.

4. Or, you could trade in the 5 and 6, and hope to match either the king or the 4s with the two cards you draw.

There is no "right" answer. But there are safer bets and long shots here. I'll get into how you calculate odds in Chapter 10.

The best way to get a feel for it is just by playing; but when you're starting, just use a simple rule of thumb—the lower the hand you aim for, the more of a chance you have of getting it. Sometimes it's better to play it safe—like saying yes to a date with a guy who you only "sort of like" instead of turning him down in hopes the millionaire hunk from the gym calls and invites you out that night. You already have a pair. It's not the best, most flashy pair, but if you risk it on a gamble for an outside chance at a more impressive hand, you may end up with less than you started with.

Considering other player's cards

Five-card draw is known as a "closed hand" game, because unlike some other poker games it doesn't have any cards exposed (or "face up") during the hand. Because of this, people often complain that you can't "read" people in five-card draw. Well, that's just bunk. You can still try to guess if your opponents are bluffing or if they've got a good hand by body language and womanly intuition. Plus, there's one golden opportunity in each hand for you to get an idea of what's behind closed doors: the draw. By watching how many cards your opponents draw, you can make a pretty good guess as to what they might have or be trying to get.

If someone draws . . .

One card—The player is either drawing to a flush or straight, or already has two pair and is hoping for a full house.

Two cards—Could be a flush or straight draw, or she's got three of a kind or a pair with another high card that she's hoping to match.

Three cards—The player either has a pair or is just keeping her two highest cards and hoping to catch a pair on the draw.

No cards—If a player "stands pat" and doesn't change a single card, she was either dealt a really high hand, or she is pretending she has one.

That's right, just like that Prada knockoff bag you got, in poker you only have to *seem* like you have the best thing going on to succeed. If other players believe you're holding something great and fold to you, you win the pot, just for being the last one standing.

Bluffing is one of the key things that makes poker as beautiful and complex a creature as you are. It's so complex itself, I had to write a whole chapter about it. Just remember for now that poker is one of the only places where lying is not only allowed, but essential. (If you can't wait, it's Chapter 9.)

✫ Variations on Five-Card Draw

Five-card draw is a game played with oodles of variations—there are a million ways to dress up this game and make it new. Four you'll often find:

Jackpots—After the cards are dealt, a player has to have a pair of jacks or better to start, or open, the betting. If no one has at least a pair of jacks, everyone folds, antes again, and a new hand is dealt from the freshly shuffled deck. You rinse and repeat as the pot grows and grows until someone gets dealt a pair of jacks or better and you can play out the hand until someone wins the jackpot.

Double draw—This is played the same as regular five-card draw, except everyone gets to draw new cards twice, and there's another round of betting to follow the second draw.

Lowball—Lowball is the same as regular five-card draw, except instead of the highest hand winning the pot, the lowest hand wins it.

Wild cards—If you're playing in a home game, wild cards may be allowed. If they are, the dealer will declare what's wild before she starts dealing. Keep in mind, when wild cards are introduced, getting five of a kind becomes possible, and the more wild cards, the more likely everyone will have ridiculously high hands.

What's great about playing five-card draw when you're first starting out is that since the rules are pretty straightforward, you can spend your energy thinking about other things: learning the ranks of hands, getting a feel for how often you'll get the winning hand, the ins and outs of betting, and starting to learn how to figure out what other people are holding. Soon enough, you'll be doing it without thinking.

SEVEN-CARD STUD

Hopefully you'll always have some studs to play with, but if you're playing a stud game, it means that there will be some cards dealt face up as well as face down to each player. And there's no drawing—the cards you are dealt are the cards you have to work with. But in seven-card stud, as the name implies, you get seven cards to use to make a five-card hand instead of only five. It's good to have options! Like packing a few different shirts to go with your favorite jeans over a weekend.

☆ How to Play Seven-Card Stud
Maximum number of players: 7

1. All players ante.
2. Each player receives two cards face down, called "hole" or "pocket" cards, and a third card face up, which is also known as "third street" or the "door" card.

3. The player with the lowest card showing "brings it in"—starts the betting. Sometimes the low-card holder must make a small, predetermined bet called a "bring-in."

4. After the betting is completed, each player receives another card. This card is "fourth street."

5. From fourth street on (the next cards dealt out are called fifth, sixth, and seventh street), the person with the highest cards showing gets the first option to bet or check.

6. After betting is completed, the fifth card is dealt face up. More betting. The sixth card is dealt face up. More betting.

7. The seventh and final card is dealt face down to each player.

8. After a final round of betting, the showdown occurs—but now players get to make their final hand out of any five cards out of the seven they were dealt. There's no obligation to use any particular card—just make the highest-ranking hand possible by picking out five from seven.

9. The highest five-card hand wins the pot.

☆Basic Strategy

The most important difference between how you play five-card draw and seven-card stud lies in the fact that in stud, you can see some of the cards the other players have, and the best thing you can do is pay attention to what's showing.

The best three cards to start with are three of a kind, pairs, and three cards in the same suit and/or in a row. Now, however, when you consider whether to raise with your three suited cards, you can look around the table and see if anyone else already has their grubby little hands on one of what you are already thinking of as "your cards." Nothing ruins the rush of seeing three lovely diamonds like seeing everyone else is showing one, too. As good as those diamonds looked at first, if three or four other players are already flashing a diamond, the chance of scoring more—enough to make a diamond flush and win a pile of money—has dropped like the stock market after the dot-com bubble burst. It might be worth it to stay in for the fourth card if the betting is light, but otherwise, it's best to toss away those pretty diamond dreams.

Once you're comfortable adjusting your own odds based on what's showing, use it to figure out what you can about your opponent's hands as well. For example, if one player is showing a 8-9-10 of different suits, it sure looks like a straight is a good possibility, and if that player's any good, she's playing it like she's got the straight already. Does she? Well, this is where all those childhood years playing Concentration pay off. If you've been paying attention, you might remember that two players folded jacks already. Looking around, you see another jack face up in someone else's hand. So you know that there's only one jack left to help your possible-straight-showing pal. If you can remember how many 6s and 7s have shown as well. . . You can see how judging a hand becomes much less a matter of guesswork. She might still have the few cards that make a straight, but it's not quite as scary a hand as it first seemed.

The final thing to remember about seven-card stud is to fold if your hand isn't good *at that very moment*. The biggest mistake beginners make with seven-card stud is to stay in for "one last card." It's easy to think that you have "four more chances" after the first deal to get lucky and get a good hand, but you'll probably have to pay to see each card. If your first three cards don't look like they're going to be the start of something good—just a bunch of low, unsuited cards, fold that crap as soon as someone makes you pay to keep it. And any badass girl knows better than to pay for garbage.

✭Variations on Seven-Card Stud

There are a lot of variations of seven-card stud played in home games, and it doesn't mean you're not a badass if you have to ask for the rules to a new one. These four are my favorites:

Chicago (also known as black Mariah)—It is dealt and played the same as traditional seven-card stud, except that this is a split-pot game. The high hand splits the pot with the player with the highest spade in the hole. The high hand and the high spade can be held by the same player, who'll "scoop" the whole delicious pot.

High-low split—In this version, the highest hand and the lowest hand split the pot. It is played the same as regular seven-card stud, except that after the seventh card is dealt and the round of betting is complete, everyone "declares" if they intend to go for a high hand or a low hand. The usual way to declare is for all the players to pick up a chip and hold it under the table, and then bring their hand back out in a closed fist over the table. All the players turn over their hands and open them at the same time. If you've got a chip in your hand, you're going high, while those with empty palms are hoping to win the low side of the hand. After everyone declares, there's an additional, final round of betting.

Follow the queen (also charmingly referred to as "follow the bitch")—This wild and crazy wildcard game is dealt the usual way, but with a fun twist. If a queen is dealt face up to any player, the following card dealt face up becomes the wild card for all players. So if I'm dealt a queen and the next gal's dealt a 5, 5s become wild for everyone. That is, until another queen comes up. . . . That's right, every time a queen is dealt face up, the wild card switches to the next card dealt face up that follows the queen. If a queen happens to be the very last card dealt face up, then guess what—all wilds are off. That's the kind of thing that gets our queen called a bitch. Some guys just can't stand a woman who changes her mind.

Baseball—In this variation, 3s and 9s are wild (for strikes and innings). But that's not all! Get a 4 face up and you get a "walk"— an extra card, dealt face down. Sometimes, based on predetermined "house rules," you will have to pay a certain amount into the pot each time you get dealt a wild card, and/or you have the option to "buy" the extra down card that comes with a 4. Usually it's the same amount as the ante. With so many possible wild cards (eight, to be exact) and the possibility of players having eight or nine cards in their hand, the showdown is usually filled with five aces beating royal flushes and full houses.

Until the explosion of hold'em, seven-card stud was the most popular card game, and it still is played in tons of home games. It's a good game for gals with good memories, and it's also played in casinos and tournaments, so it's a game you can transition from "evening in" to "evening out" without a lot of fuss.

TEXAS HOLD'EM

The man who won the first two World Series of Poker, Johnny Moss, once said, "Hold'em is to stud and draw what chess is to checkers," and many call it "the Cadillac of Poker." If five-card stud is the poker of movies, then Texas hold'em is unquestionably the poker of television. The "World Poker Tour" on the Travel Channel, "The World Series of Poker" on ESPN, and the fun-filled, light-hearted "Celebrity Poker Showdown" on Bravo have undoubtedly fueled the fire that has made poker red hot. The biggest difference between Texas hold'em and draw and stud games is the element of community cards. You see, in the other games everyone is playing with their very own special set of cards, but in hold'em, the kids all have to share. But you don't have to play nice.

☆How to Play Texas Hold'em

Maximum number of players: 11 (Technically, you can play a single hand of hold'em with 22 people, but after 12 it just becomes silly. Usually it's played with 7 to 10 people.)

1. The two players to the left of the dealer put out *blind bets*.
2. Every player is dealt two cards, face down, called the hole/ pocket cards.
3. The action falls on the player to the left of the big blind. She can either call the bet, raise it, or fold. Betting continues around the table.
4. After the betting is complete, three cards are dealt face up in the center of the table, which is referred to as the

"board." The first three cards are called "the flop." These cards are "community cards," meaning everyone can (and will) use them in combination with their own hole cards to make the best hand. Before the dealer deals out the flop, she first deals one card face down, a "burn" card.

5. From the flop on, betting begins with the player to the dealer's left, who can check or bet.

6. The dealer again "burns" a card, and then deals a fourth card face up on the board. This is called "fourth street," or "the turn card."

7. There is another round of betting.

8. The dealer "burns and turns" another card. The final card is called "fifth street," or "the river."

9. A final round of betting occurs. The remaining players show their cards and the person who can make the best five-card hand by combining their pocket cards with the cards on the board wins. (In some rare cases, the five cards making up the board will actually be the best hand, in which case everyone left in the hand divides up the pot.)

⋆ Basic Strategy

There's a reason that hold'em is "the Pink Cadillac of Poker." There are more books written on how to win at hold'em than any other poker game, some hundreds and hundreds of pages long on the intricacies of how to act in every possible situation. I cover some of the strategies in Section 3, but before you get to calculating odds and bullying with bets, you need to get a good grip on a few basic considerations.

Here are the three most important things to think about:

1. What's in the hole?

In hold'em, the most important decision comes when you look at your hole cards. These two cards are the only things that are unique to you—the only secret that's just yours. It's these two cards that will make the difference in every hand. It turns out most hands aren't worth playing. To paint it with the largest brush, the best hands are pairs and two cards 10 and higher, especially if those two cards are in the same suit.

To break it down a little more, look at this list of best starting hands—often referred to as "premium hands"—in rough order from best to worst:

High pairs: A-A, K-K, Q-Q, J-J
A-K; suited and unsuited
K-Q, A-Q, Q-J, J-10, A-J; suited

I almost always play all of the above hands no matter where I am in relation to the dealer. If I'm in a late-betting position—meaning I'm either the dealer or in the two seats to the right of the dealer—or the betting is very light before the flop, I'll also stay in with other good-but-not-fantastic hands, including:

10-10, 9-9, 8-8
Any two cards 10 and higher; suited
Suited connectors, such as 5-6 of hearts or 8-9 of clubs
A-10, K-Q, K-J, K-10, Q-J, Q-10, J-10; unsuited

All the low pairs
Ace plus any card of the same suit

If you're in a game with light betting before the flop, you can start out with the more iffy hands. It also depends on how many people are in the game. The more people you're playing with, the better your starting hand has to be. If you're playing "short-handed," meaning with five or fewer, you can play more marginal hands. To put it in perspective, if you're playing ten-handed (you plus nine others), the odds are greater that one of you *will* get dealt an ace than that no one will get one, so you've got to raise your standards for what you'll start with.

2. The flop should fit your hand.

There's an old saying about the flop: "Fit or Fold." Just like you should fold up your skinny jeans at the bottom of your drawer if you gain weight, if the flop comes and it doesn't improve your hand, you should get out. This is especially important if you played one of those "iffy" or marginal hands.

After the flop, you've seen five out of the seven cards you're going to—that's about 70 percent of the hand. If you were hoping for a heart flush and no hearts come, it's over for you—you can't possibly get it now. If you stayed in with a low pair, say 4s, and the flop is all face cards, get out. Someone's got one of those face cards in the pocket and a higher pair than you. On the other hand, if the flop came with a 4, you'd have a sneaky set of 4s that could win you a monster pot.

3. Figure out what hands are possible that could beat yours.

The beauty and intricacy of hold'em lies in the magic of the community cards. Unlike draw or stud, in hold'em you know exactly what cards everyone else is working with—the same ones as you. All the players are going to have to use at least three of the community cards to form their final hand. This gives you a lot of information you can use to decide what other players might be holding.

Look at the cards on the board and puzzle together what hands are possible. The other thing that changes in community card games is that for every board, there are always two cards that will give someone the absolute, unbeatable, best possible hand. To give an easy example of what I mean by this, if the board showed 2 ♣ 9 ♣ 10 ♦ J ♦ K ♦, the best possible hand would be made if someone had the queen and ace of diamonds in her hand, giving her a royal straight flush. You want to look at the community cards at the flop, turn, and river, and figure out what two cards, at that moment, would make the unbeatable hand, which is known as "the nuts."

To demonstrate the game and why these are the three most key elements to the game, let's look at a sample hand with six players. I'm going to assume everyone stayed in until the end, even if they shouldn't have.

Player 1: A ♣ K ♠
Player 2: J ♦ J ♥
Player 3: 7 ♠ 2 ♥

Player 4: A ♦ 4 ♦
Player 5: Q ♦ 6 ♥
Player 6: 9 ♣ 8 ♣
Flop: A ♠ Q ♣ 7 ♣ Turn: 6 ♦ River: K ♣

What does everyone have?

Player 1: Two pair, aces and kings
Player 2: Pair of jacks, with the ace on the board for a kicker
Player 3: Pair of 7s, with the ace kicker
Player 4: Pair of aces, with the king on the board as a kicker
Player 5: Two pair, queens and 6s
Player 6: A club flush

Player 6 takes it. Although in this example, the strongest starting hand didn't win, this hand still demonstrates a lot of the important principles.

Who should've stayed in for the flop?
I've seen people play every one of these hands, including the 7-2 off-suit, which is the worst possible starting hand in hold'em because it can't even make a low straight, no matter what the board shows. But that's an easy preflop fold. The A-K, J-J, and 9-8 are all playable hands. The most questionable hand here is the Q-6. It seems like a good hand, what with that pretty lady smiling at you and all, but it's truly not. But with both the Q-6 and the A-4, you might stay in if it's cheap to do so.

Who and how did the flop fit?

When the flop came A-Q-7, it was time for the J-J to fold. Same for the Q-6. Sure, she made a pair, but it wasn't the highest pair on the board. Unless everyone checks and you truly think that no one has an ace, these two hands should be tossed away now. Even though a pair of jacks is a pretty strong starting hand, chances are someone's in there with an ace or queen, so any pair you've got lower than that is garbage now.

On the other hand, the two players with aces are going to be happy, as is the 9-8 of clubs, since she's got four cards to a flush. But note: If the flop had come without a single club, the 9-8 would have become worthless and been folded. And those players with aces? Well, one of those ace hands (A-K) has already beat the other (A-4)—and that's the trouble with hole cards consisting of aces and a low card. Another player is likely waiting to kick your ace's behind with her higher kicker.

What could other people have?

The final lesson here is to remember to consider what the best possible hand is on the board. The A-K, if she didn't look closely, might be excited to have made the top two pair on the river. But what that king of clubs also did was make a flush possible. And, in fact, that's exactly what happened.

Quiz: Forget the hands everyone was dealt and just look at the board from the example hand. What two pocket cards would have been unbeatable?

Answer: The ace of clubs and any other club, creating the highest possible flush.

BADASS'S BRIEF GUIDE TO OTHER COMMUNITY CARD GAMES

Each of these games is similar to hold'em in that they all have five community cards that players can use to make their hand, and the five board cards are dealt in the same way, with a flop, turn, and river. The betting follows the same pattern as well. You won't run into these games as much as you tour the tables, but they're fun to add to your arsenal. You don't really *need* that red satin cocktail dress that's on sale, but you never know—you could be invited to a gala benefit at the last minute!

✮ Omaha (High)

Omaha is almost exactly like Texas hold'em, except with two differences:

1. You get dealt four hole cards to start with instead of two.
2. Your final hand must be made up of exactly two cards from the hole and three from the board.

What you need to remember if you're playing Omaha is that the hands that will win are *much* higher than in Texas hold'em. With double the cards in the pocket to pick from, you'll always have something—like rooming with a girlfriend who's the same size as you. Your closets overfloweth. It seems like you'll always be the best dressed, have a fabulous hand. But remember, everyone else just doubled their card wardrobe as well, and a pair of anything, even aces, will rarely win. Two pair also aren't worth much. Straights, flushes, and full houses beat each other routinely in Omaha.

The other thing to remember is the fact that you must use only two cards from your hand and only three from the board, no more, no less. Think of it as the limit to that roommate's generosity: she'll let you borrow shoes and a top, but not a skirt and a scarf as well.

How does this change the game?

Let's say you're dealt: A ♣ K ♠ 6 ♦ 5 ♦

And the board is: A ♠ Q ♠ 7 ♠ 3 ♠ 2 ♣

If it were hold'em, you'd be thrilled—you could use the king of spades with the spades on the board and you'd have the best possible flush. But not in Omaha. Since you have to use two of your pocket cards, you've got nothing. All you've got is a pair of lousy aces. It can be frustrating—like all you wanted to borrow was your roommate's fabulous Gucci blouse, but she wouldn't let you wear it unless you also agreed to don her hideous acid-washed jeans.

A final example: Three of a kind in the hole becomes bad news for you since the best you can hope for is that the another of that rank comes on the board, so you can actually have three of a kind. But unless there's also a pair on the board (giving you a full house), a plain old three of a kind is still unlikely to be the winning hand in Omaha. Omaha's the only game in town where being dealt four of a kind will make a woman cry tears of woe instead of joy.

✯Omaha Hi-Lo and Omaha 8

Omaha is most often played a hi-lo game, with the lowest hand splitting the pot with the highest hand. In Omaha hi-lo, the lowest hand is always A-2-3-4-5. Most people play what's known as Omaha 8-or-better hi-lo, commonly called just Omaha 8. The "8-or-better" part means that a low hand cannot have a card higher than 8 in it. So an A-2-4-5-9 doesn't qualify as a low. If there's no low hand, the high hand takes the whole pot.

Here's the biggest twist with this game: You still have to use two cards from the hole and three from the board, but you can make and play two different hands, a high and a low hand. What that means is if your pocket cards are A ♣ A ♦ 2 ♦ 3 ♣ (considered the best starting hand in Omaha 8), you can use that A-A to make a high hand, and the A-2 to make a low hand.

⭐Pineapple

In pineapple—sometimes called "crazy pineapple"—each player is dealt three hole cards to begin. After the flop, though, each player has to choose one of her hole cards to discard. After that, the game is the same as Texas hold'em, with players making the best hand from the two hole cards they've kept and the five on the board. It's sort of Texas hold'em with a free rental card—like the cards are just so happy to have you play with them, they'll give you an extra one to borrow for a little while, but not to keep.

FABULOUS AT THE FELT: TABLE MANNERS

Manners are a sensitive awareness of the feelings of others. If you have
that awareness, you have good manners, no matter which fork you use.
—EMILY POST

ou may be a savvy, smart gal who knows which fork to
use for each course in a fancy restaurant, who *always*
writes thank-you notes on time, and who never shows up
late for an appointment, but Miss Manners isn't going to help you
when you sit down at the felt. That's not to say there isn't a poker
protocol! Just as you wouldn't dare to show up at a dinner party
without a nice bottle of wine or flowers, you shouldn't sit down at
a poker table without mastering the basic etiquette. You want to
be known as a badass for your playing skills and your table attitude, not as a pain in the ass who turns a good game bad.

Whether you're playing at a home game or in a casino, poker
is more fun when everyone follows the rules. It keeps the game
running smoothly as your fresh-shaven legs and lets everyone

concentrate on the action at hand. Learn these do's and don'ts and the boys will hold the door to poker open for you forever.

DON'T . . .

Keep them waiting—When meeting a date, it's standard to show up ten minutes late, but at the poker table, you're not just making one guy wait. To those five guys waiting for you to bet or fold, each moment is a lifetime—worse than if they were standing around, holding your purse while you shop for shoes. This isn't the way to play it here. When the action is on you, make your move quickly.

Make a mess—You know how in the movies they're always tossing their chips willy-nilly into the pile at the center? Well, in real life, they call this "splashing the pot" and it's a definite no-no. It makes it hard to see how much you've bet. Just stack up your chips neatly like a lady would and put them out there.

Show your cards—When a hand is still being played, it is *essential* that you don't show your cards to anyone. Make sure no one can see them when you fold and don't talk about what cards you held. Even if you are sitting next to a cutie who wants to commiserate on the garbage he's been getting for hands all night, it's bad form to do so, and if anyone who's still in the hand overhears, it gives that player an unfair advantage.

DO . . .

Wait your turn—Betting or folding before it's your turn is one of the seven deadly sins of poker. It gives an unfair edge to any player who hasn't acted yet and will annoy the people who've already bet. And if you're so eager to bet that you can't wait your turn, you're only hurting yourself by giving away the fact you've got good cards.

Leave it on the table—Your cards should *always* remain in plain view. In fact, in most games (other than five-card draw), your cards should never leave the table. That means no picking up those hole cards and pressing them to your chest. You probably won't hear any complaints from the cards, but your fellow players might grumble. It's good practice to leave your chips on the table, too.

Share with everyone—Sometimes after a hand is over, you're just dying to share what cards you folded, like you've just got your hands on a hot piece of gossip. It happens to everyone. You know you *shouldn't* share but . . . it's too good to keep to yourself. If you do decide to show your cards, though, you have to show them to the whole table. It's only fair, and that way no one feels left out of the secret.

Be a good loser and better winner—Nobody likes a whiner or a braggart. Take your losses gracefully and your wins humbly. Inside, you may feel like jumping up and doing a victory dance, but a sweet smile coupled with a shrug and, "I guess it's just lady luck," will win you good will on top of the pot.

RAKES, COWBOYS, AND ROUNDERS: TALKING THE TALK

I just realized something. Joker is poker with a j . . . coincidence?
—PHOEBE, ON *FRIENDS*

The poker table may be the only place a broad gets to say, "I've got the nuts," and have everyone understand and agree with her. How can you not love that? Just like the English speak a slightly different language than the Americans, the poker player has a dialect as well. Just as the Eskimos have all those words for snow, the Pokertablians have created hundreds of words to describe cards more precisely. And more colorfully.

Even if you're too "mature" or whatever to still enjoy any opportunity to say "nuts," if you're going to follow the action and fit in in the land of Pokertablia, you need to bone up on the terms. You don't want to lose a stud's respect because when he says he's got a "wired pair" you think he's talking about some new gadget.

VITAL VOCAB FOR ALL VIXENS

If you're not a lover of lingo, just familiarize yourself with the terms in this section. They're the ones you need to know to not get beat up on the poker playground.

Action—Used a few ways: if the game's stalled, someone might ask, "Where's the action?"—they're asking whose turn it is to bet. If it's your turn, they'll tell you, "The action's on you." Or it's used to describe the betting itself. "The game has a lot of action," means there's a lot of betting and money changing hands.

Bad beat—When a really good hand is beaten by an even better hand, like in the movie *Honeymoon in Vegas*, when Nick Cage's character has his 7-8-9-10-J straight flush beaten by James Caan's 8-9-10-J-Q straight flush. Especially used in hold'em when a hand that is favored to win is beat because the other, weaker hand got a lucky card on the river. For example, if you have A-K against 5-4 and the flop is A-K-5, the only thing that could make the 5-4 the winning hand at this point is one of the two 5s left, and a smart player would get out. But if Mr. 5-4 stays in and does get that 5, your two pair will be beaten by his three of a kind. Badly.

Bump—To raise. "Bump it to fifty" means raise the total bet to $50. Also see "kick it."

Burn—In hold'em and Omaha, the dealer discards the top card, face down, before turning up the three-card flop. The discarded card is the "burn card." The dealer burns a card before dealing fourth and fifth streets as well. It's supposed to prevent cheating even if the deck is marked, since the cheaters won't be able to read the markings on that top card and use the information to their advantage.

Button—A round marker used to show who the dealer is in a hand. It's always used when there's a pro dealing, but many home games use one as well so it's clear to everyone who's dealing. Also called a "buck."

Family pot—Sometimes everyone just wants to play! When everyone (or almost everyone) at the table stays in a hand, you've got a happy family pot.

Heads up—When a hand or game comes down to just two players. Also called "head to head."

Kick it—Raise the bet. If you're raising a $10 bet by another $10, you'd say, "Kick it up to $20."

Limp—To bet the minimum or simply call. In hold'em, when the little blind simply meets the big blind bet as opposed to raising, the little blind is "limping in."

Muck—As a noun, a discarded hand, or the pile of discarded hands. As a verb, to fold your hand.

Nut—The best possible hand in games with community cards is called "the nuts." Also used with a particular hand, such as "the nut straight" or "the nut flush"—meaning not only do you have a flush, you've got the unbeatable flush.

Position—Where you sit in the order of betting during a hand of poker. The players who are first to act are said to be in early position, and the last ones to act are in late positions. Also used as a verb: if another player gets to act after you, she's got position on you.

Post—To put in a bet. Usually this refers to a forced bet, like a blind. If you had stepped away from the table for a bathroom break someone might "post" your blind for you.

Rabbit hunting—When a hand ends with a player winning the pot before the cards are fully dealt out, one of the players who folded during play might ask the dealer to show her what cards would have come up if she'd stayed in the hand and all the cards had been dealt out. This is called "rabbit hunting."

Rake—A fee charged by the house to play. Also called "chop."

Riffle—To shuffle your chips.

Roll—To deal a card face up, as in "Roll the next card."

Stack—Your total chips on the table. If you've got fewer chips than most other players, you're "short stacked."

Tilt—When a player lets her emotions affect her play negatively. Often after losing, a player will go "on tilt" and make poor decisions. It's the same problem that causes a woman to have sex with her ex.

Toke—A tip, usually for the dealer. Comes from *token*, as in "a token of appreciation."

Under the gun—The first player to act in a hand is said to be "under the gun."

NICKNAMES FOR THE PEOPLE IN YOUR POKER NEIGHBORHOOD

Calling station—A player who calls every bet no matter what, often saying things such as "to keep you honest." Also see "fish."

Dog—The underdog to win a hand.

Fish—A sucker. A bad or weak player. Also called "pigeons" and "donkeys."

Mechanic—A cheat. A card manipulator. A bottom-dealer.

Prop player—A player who's paid by the house to play, but plays the game itself with her own money.

Railbird—Someone who's just watching. In casinos, spectators have to watch from behind a rail to prevent cheating and distraction.

Rock—An extremely conservative player who plays only the best hands. A "tight" player.

Rounder—An expert at cards and the poker world; someone who plays for a living.

Shill—A player who's playing for the house, with the house's money.

COOL THINGS TO CALL CARDS AND HANDS

Baby—A small card, like 2 or 5. Usually used for 6 or lower.

Belly buster—A straight draw that's missing one card inside the numerical sequence, such as 3-4-6-7. Also called a "gutshot draw" or "inside straight draw."

Bicycle—An ace-low straight: A-2-3-4-5. Also called a "bike" or "wheel."

Boat—A full house. Also called a "barn."

Connectors—Two consecutive cards, like 8-9 or J-Q.

Dead—A dead card or hand is one that is no longer in play. You can also be "drawing dead," which means that no matter what card comes, you'll still lose. It is hopeless, like wishing that your hot guy friend wasn't gay and would fall madly in love with you.

Dead man's hand—Two pair made up of aces and 8s. It's legendary because it was the hand held by Old West legend "Wild Bill" Hickok when he was shot dead.

Deuce—A 2. Also called a "duck."

Knave—Jacks. Also called "johnnies" or "hooks."

Motown—Two pair made up of jacks and 5s. Say it fast—easy as ABC, 123 to remember.

Open-ended straight—Four consecutive cards, like 4-5-6-7, that will become a straight if you hit the card at either end—in this case, a 3 or 8.

Outs—The number of cards that will improve your hand. It's better to have as many outs as possible.

Overpair—If you've got a pair in the hole higher than any in the flop, you've got an overpair—for example, if the flop is 7-9-J and you're holding a pair of aces.

Paint—Face cards (jacks, queens, and kings). Also called "court cards."

Penulti-nuts—A really good hand that still ends up second-best. Holding the "penulti-nut" hand often leads to a bad beat.

Quads—Four of a kind.

Rags—A series of unsuited low cards. Also called "blanks." As in, you're shooting blanks.

Rainbow—A flop that holds three different suits.

Rolled up—When in seven-card stud, your first three cards are three of a kind. Also called "rollers" or "roll-ups."

Set—In flop games, if you've got a pair in the hole and another card of the same rank appears on the board, you have a set. If you hit your three of a kind on the flop, you've "flopped a set."

Suicide king—The king of hearts, whose traditional drawing has a sword at his own head.

Toilet paper—What's easier to throw away than toilet paper? A totally worthless, easy to fold hand.

Top pair—When a card in your hand pairs the top card on the board.

Trey—A 3.

Trips—When you make three of a kind by matching one card in your hand with two on the board.

Underpair—The opposite of overpair. If you're holding 3-3 and the flop comes A-10-7, your pair is now lower than any made with the community cards. Your 3s are an underpair.

Up—When someone says they have "aces up" it means she has two pair, and the higher pair are aces. Jacks up would be two pair with jacks being the higher pair, etc.

Wired—If you're dealt a pair in the hole in seven-card stud, it's called a wired pair.

SLANG FOR STARTING HANDS IN HOLD'EM

AA—American Airlines, bullets, pocket rockets, sticks

AJ—Ajax

AK—Big slick

KJ—Kojak

KK—Cowboys

K9—Canine

QJ—Maverick, Oedipus Rex

QQ—Dames, ladies, four tits

Q ♠ 5 ♠—Granny Mae (Superstition says this hand has a mysterious power that will reward you if you bet on it.)

Q3—A San Francisco Busboy (a queen with a trey—ha, ha)

J ♣ 9 ♣—If both cards are clubs, it's called a T. J. Cloutier

10-2—Doyle Brunson (He won two World Series of Poker titles with this hand.)

5-4—Jesse James, for his Colt .45

A MIND-NUMBING FLU MAKES YOU MISS YOUR REGULAR GAME. Your car breaks down on your way to the casino. Or you just need to give your bankroll a little break. But you've still got the hankering for a piece of the poker action. When you can't join 'em, you can watch 'em. Learn about the lore of Las Vegas in movies like *Bugsy,* or board a bus to Atlantic City and see how far a gambling addict will go with *Owning Mahowny*. Interested in seeing a slice of the modern poker scene? *Rounders* has hold'em, underground clubs, *and* Matt Damon and Edward Norton. You want singing and dancing? *Viva Las Vegas!* Add guns and gangsters and you've got *Guys and Dolls.* And if your fever's running really, really high, I recommend the French film that led in the New Wave cinema movement of the 1960s, *Bob Le Flambeur* (Bob the Gambler, or High Roller). Like *The Sting* or *Ocean's 11,* the movie focuses on a grand scheme, but in a very black-and-white—how do you say—French way.

5 Vegas Lives:
Bugsy
Casino
Honeymoon in Vegas
Ocean's 11
Viva Las Vegas

6 Poker Flicks:
A Big Hand for a Little Lady
California Split
The Cincinnati Kid
Maverick
Rounders
The Sting

9 Fine Gambling Films:
Bob Le Flambeur
The Cooler
Croupier
The Gambler
Guys and Dolls
Hard Eight
The Hustler
Lock, Stock and Two Smoking Barrels
Owning Mahowny

SECTION TWO

SHUFFLE UP AND DEAL

If you can't spot the sucker in the first half hour at the table, then it's you.

—ANONYMOUS

QUEEN OF CLUBS:
SETTING UP A GIRLS' POKER NIGHT

Sex is good, but poker lasts longer.
—ANONYMOUS

Badass girls gather in book clubs, knitting circles, and, back in the day, to watch *Sex and the City*. I like all-girl gatherings. Whether it's for afternoon tea and crumpets or a pajama party in someone's house where someone tries to sell you sex toys like they were Tupperware, be there. Without men, nobody is worried about if her hair looks good or if some guy is looking at her. You can slouch. You can belch and fart, and then just laugh about it as you gossip and pour out another shaker of mojitos.

There's no better way to spend a night with a group of your girlfriends than playing cards. It's also a marvelous method to bring your different groups of gal pals together and really get to know one another—there's something about the table that sparks the best conversations. The atmosphere is both full of energy and relaxed and open—though the cocktails may have something to do with that, too. Since everyone is in the same game, everyone interacts. Even if you throw a two- or three-table poker extravaganza, everyone will at least get to know the others at that particular poker table. Unlike a dinner party, where people often pair off to talk, with poker, you have to talk to everyone at some point as you call and raise and bet. There may be side conversations, but the central one happens around the clatter of chips and the riffling of cards. There's also something about going head to head with someone that builds a bond, even though one of you will end up the loser.

Unlike book clubs, there's no reading required, so your friends who don't have time to read a whole book in a month have no excuse. Your girlfriends don't have to invest in anything before like yarn or needles or fabric; they just have to show up. Plus, it's easy to teach the basics to ladies who've never played before, and it is a low-stress way to practice poker skills. And whether you have one once a week or once a month, it begins a beautifully badass tradition that may last for years.

GET THIS PARTY STARTED RIGHT

First you'll have to figure out how many people to invite. My ideal number for a night of poker is a lucky party of seven. It allows for just enough cards to play seven-card stud, but still is a good amount for hold'em to be interesting. You can fit seven or eight people around most dining-room tables, and with seven, there are enough people around so you don't feel like you're just pushing the chips back and forth between the same few people. In my opinion, five is the minimum, but four can still have a good time. If you've only got one table, cap the guest list at ten.

Pick a date and time and send those invites out, either by e-mail, phone, or use an Internet-based invitation like Evite *(www. evite.com)*. What's nice about using Evite is you can see how many people have responded and easily invite a couple more if you're short-handed.

✴ Supplies to Set the Scene
Essential:

Two decks of cards

Enough chips for everyone—a good rule of thumb is at least thirty per player, ten each in three different colors.

A big table and enough chairs

Highly recommended:

A dealer button

Kickass tunes (see recommended playlists, pp. 63, 73, 131, 155)

Finger foods: Chips, pretzels, veggies and dip, popcorn, licorice whips

Beverages: Beer, wine, soda, water, killer cocktails

If you want a change from cosmos and gimlets, why not use those martini glasses to serve up a poker cocktail to the chicks?

Poker Cocktail
1 ounce sweet vermouth   1 ounce light rum
Shake it up with ice and pour it into lime-garnished glasses.

HOW MUCH MONEY ARE WE TALKING ABOUT HERE?

You'll want to let the let the ladies know how much dough to bring when you invite them. The trick to is to find an amount that's meaningful for everyone, but not so much that people start thinking about how they won't be able to afford to get those highlights after all. It has to be enough money so it matters but it shouldn't be so much that losing the entire buy-in will mean skipping paying the electric bill.

A good rule of thumb is to think of it in terms of what you and your friends would each spend if you went out for a Friday night on the town. If you're a college student playing with pals, you probably don't want to lose more than $20 in a night—you need that gas to get to class. On the other hand, if your friends are city girls used to hanging out with the glamouratti, most of those molls won't blink an eye at $40 to $100. Believe me, in New York City, the land of $12 martinis, $50 for a full evening of fun seems like a bargain.

To make sure money matters don't become a mess, lay out the following for the ladies:

- **What's the buy-in?** (How much moolah should each babe bring?)
- **What's the betting structure and stakes?** (Is it a spread limit, fixed limit, etc.? How much can players bet/raise each round? Is there a maximum bet? Are you playing with antes or blinds? How much are they?)
- **Is check-raising allowed?** (Check-raising is when a player

checks, hoping someone will bet after her so she can raise when the betting comes back to her.)

- **Are there a maximum number of raises?** (Most games "cap," or stop, the betting after three or four raises each round.)
- **What about when it's head to head?** (If a hand is narrowed so it's one against one, the two remaining players are often allowed to keep raising each other indefinitely.)

YOUR HOUSE, YOUR RULES

There are a few decisions about the rules of the night's game you need to make before you begin. Once everyone's there and ready to shuffle up and deal, make sure you've made everything in this list clear:

- Are wild cards allowed?
- What is the lowest hand?
- How will you declare if you are going high or low in those games where it applies?
- Who's responsible for shuffling the previous hand? (If someone's not good at shuffling, have a few people be on shuffle duty all night rather than rotate it.)
- Who cuts the cards? Will you even bother?
- What, if anything, constitutes a misdeal?
- Will the game be dealer's choice, a rotation game, or one game only?

DEALER'S CHOICE VS. ROTATION GAMES VS. ONE GAME ONLY

In "dealer's choice," the deal rotates to the left after each hand and each new dealer chooses what game will be played next. This is what most home games do—it allows each person to choose what she feels like playing at that moment, either by what she's best at or just what she enjoys playing most. If your aim is to laugh all night and have the most fun, deal yourself in for choice.

In a "rotation game," while the deal still rotates after each hand, you play one game for a full round, until the deal returns to the first dealer. You pick which games are to be rotated before starting. A lineup might be as follows: seven-card stud, hold'em, five-card draw, Omaha. The betting structure remains constant, no matter what game is being played. This is a good choice if most of the women know their way around the table and want to practice a few different games.

"One game only" is just what it sounds like. In my regular home game, it's hold'em all night long. The only change we make is that sometimes the last hour we change the limits—we go from limit to pot-limit hold'em. This is best for ladies who have been hooked by poker on TV or more serious poker players.

LET THE GOOD TIMES ROLL

Dim the lights, turn on the tunes, and make sure everyone's got something to drink. There's no question that people feel better about losing if they can do so in style, and feel like they've had a pleasant evening out.

If you've gathered a group that doesn't know each other very well, get the girls gabbing by adding an extra nonpoker element of game play to the evening. For instance, as guests arrive, tape the names of famous females to their backs and have them try to guess what celeb they've got by asking questions of other players. Or add a different dimension of deception by playing "truth from lies," where each woman states two things about herself that are true and one that's false and everyone else tries to figure out which is which. Not only is it a way for everyone to see who's a skilled liar, but you'll also learn some interesting tidbits about your guests. The downside of both of these is they'll probably slow down the game, and, after all, you are there to play poker. Definitely don't try doing both in the same evening. If you want to keep the game running relatively smoothly, there are other ways to add some sass.

☆ Six Fast Ways to Add Femme Flair

1. Pass around a tiara instead of a dealer button to show who's dealing.
2. Play with fun decks—go high-brow with an artsy deck or break out the beefcake with some Chippendale-style cards.
3. Challenge the chicks to come up with new nicknames for hands and hole cards—call a pair of kings the Wilson brothers after Owen and Luke, or refer to jacks by the names of your exes.
4. Award a prize for the worst beat of the night—good chocolate always soothes a bruised babe's ego.

5. Have all the guests create a poker nickname for themselves or make inventing new monikers a group effort.
6. Offer props and accessories—visors, wigs, boas, dark sunglasses, cigarette holders, lucky charms—for the ladies to take with them to the table.

Whether you choose to add extra entertainment or just play it straight, odds are in your favor that everyone will have a winning time.

EXTRA CREDIT

BADASS PLAYLIST #1

CLUB LADIES NIGHT

COME TO WHERE POKER BLENDS WITH PARTYING. A PLACE WHERE money-filled melodies meet rocking riot girl tunes, with a side of soul and dash of all-time gambling greats. It's the perfect playlist to get the girls going.

So let's get this party started—quickly!

1. "5 O'clock in the Morning"—The Donnas
2. "All I Wanna Do"—Sheryl Crow
3. "Big Payback"—James Brown
4. "Deal"—Grateful Dead
5. "Easy Money"—Rickie Lee Jones
6. "For the Love of Money"—The O'Jays
7. "The Gambler"—Kenny Rogers
8. "Go Down Gambling"—Blood, Sweat & Tears
9. "Ladies Night"—Lil' Kim, TLC, and Missy Elliot (the original Kool and the Gang version works, too)
10. "Lily, Rosemary, and the Jack of Hearts"—Bob Dylan
11. "Luck Be a Lady"—Frank Loesser

12. "My Favorite Game"—Cardigans
13. "Queen of Hearts"—Juice Newton

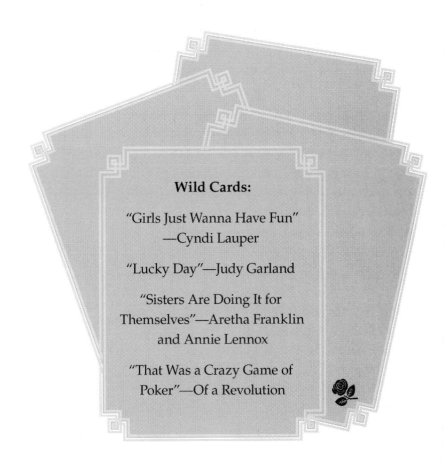

Wild Cards:

"Girls Just Wanna Have Fun"
—Cyndi Lauper

"Lucky Day"—Judy Garland

"Sisters Are Doing It for
Themselves"—Aretha Franklin
and Annie Lennox

"That Was a Crazy Game of
Poker"—Of a Revolution

LADIES IN HIGH SOCIETY: GETTING INTO THE BOYS' GAME

Men are like a deck of cards.
You'll find the occasional king, but most are jacks.

—LAURA SWENSON

While most girls gab over books and set off on shopping expeditions, guys get together to watch sports, tee off at the golf course, take in some topless entertainment, and play poker. The traditional boys' night out is often viewed as a sacred time, when boys can be bad boys and enjoy some serious male bonding over beers at the bars. It's the only time, they claim, they can really let loose and be themselves—without women to watch them be the ball-scratching, swearing, sweaty beasts they are.

A poker game is usually just the guys, playing in someone's house, sitting around a table all night together. The image comes to mind of a group of middle-aged guys, neckties loosened from unbuttoned collars, sitting in a basement around an old card table, complete with cigar smoke curling through the beam of the bare bulb lighting the room. Games that have gone on once a week for years. Decades.

While, of course, that kind of boy's game exists, it's not the only game in town. Besides, it's not like the game you're dying to get into is with men your father's age. (And if that does happen do be your thing, don't worry, there are still ways to get into the game.) With the boom in poker over the last few years, there are games going on all over the place with men of all ages; even teenage boys are gathering together to play poker. The good news is, the younger the players and the newer the game, the more likely they'll be open to having a woman sit down across from them. In my experience, most guys are happy to have a girl play with them, as long as she doesn't mind being in the minority, gender-wise, and doesn't expect them to behave on her account. There's also a novelty to women players, which many men find appealing—what a lark! A girl at the game! What fun! Men generally view women as poor poker players, and a sucker is always welcome at most games.

That said, there may be resistance—you may hear:

1. "It'll ruin the atmosphere. It's a guy's night."
2. "It's not a 'fun' game; we play serious poker."
3. "I wouldn't mind, but 'so and so' really doesn't want women."
4. "We're full."
5. "None of the other guys' girlfriends play. It'd be weird."

TURNING THOSE NO'S INTO HELLO'S

1. "It'll ruin the atmosphere. It's a guy's night."

Some men think that adding a woman to the table is as good as setting up a direct feed to their significant other's room. They won't be able to be the swearing, smoking, drunk, tits-loving men they really are. They don't want ladies at the lodge! The locker room is off-limits! Besides, they'll tell you, you wouldn't like it. It's no place for a lady. Your best strategy here is to convince them that you're used to being around the worst of men, and even enjoy it—whether it's by talking about out-farting your three brothers, spilling out anecdotes of accompanying former flames to strip joints, or being the only broad on your local bar's dart team. Reassure them you've been to tons of similar poker nights before where you were the lone woman ranger. Say you'll bring midget porn (don't worry, they won't hold you to it). The point is to be lighthearted and sort of crude. Once there, remember you have to live up to your promises and adapt to their rules—if you try and tame their game, you'll find yourself uninvited.

2. "It's not a 'fun' game; we play serious poker."

They think you, being a woman, can't play. They play serious poker and since you must suck, you'll ruin the game. This one's the easiest to crack, since you, of course, are no slouch at the table; you're well versed in the vernacular and well-rounded in your game knowledge. Just start talking the talk—ask what they play, for what stakes. Just like at a job interview, impress them by asking further questions—if he says, "Three-six Omaha," ask, "Omaha high or eight?" Relate stories about some of the games you've played and how long you've been playing (embellishing is acceptable). Once you're invited, make sure to bone up on any games you've overexaggerated your prowess at.

3. "I wouldn't mind, but 'so and so' really doesn't want women."

Ah, the old "it isn't me . . . it's him!" excuse. They'd rather not have you themselves, but they don't want to be dicks and flat-out say no. So they pass the "no" buck to some other guy in the game. They're also hoping you'll just give up and forget. Don't. Be persistent and available. Unlike dating, it's not sad and pathetic to keep asking the same guy the same question when it comes to getting into a poker game. It may be annoying, sure, but the squeaky wheel . . . Meanwhile, try to talk poker and other guy-tailored topics with your male associate. After he sees what kind of guy's gal you are, the objection will likely slip away. If there really is a guy who doth protest, try to meet him in another social situation and work your charms. Once you've got one of these guys on your side, it's much easier to make the objections of the rest fall like dominoes. Convince them there's no harm and if they try it, they just might like it.

4. "We're full."

He looks at you and stoically tells you there's no room at the inn, or that the game's on hiatus. First, figure out if it's true—it may very well be. Regardless, it's as good as full for your purposes. But even this game isn't unbreakable—though it'll probably take some patience. Every once in a while, most games need an extra player in the game—someone goes on vacation or has to work late or attend his kid's recital. Let them know you're available if they ever need an extra player or someone to fill in a seat. Meanwhile, when opportunity presents, let them overhear you talk about other games you play in. Engage them in talk about the latest tournament on TV. If you're really determined, try to find out if any of the players attend other games that would be easier to get invited to, and play there. After he sees you playing for real, he'll be more likely to consider you when, in fact, the game does have a space. And if you happen to lose a few pots to the guy, he may peg you for a fish he and his buddies can take for all her money. No harm in him thinking that.

5. "None of the other guys' girlfriends play. It'd be weird."

If the object of your desire is to go with your boyfriend to his once-a-week games, it's a tricky situation. Whether or not a girlfriend has ever entered this poker room, you can be pretty sure no girlfriend of his ever has. The first step, if it hasn't happened already, is to find a way to play poker with your significant other. Suggest a weekend getaway to a casino, or organize a poker game at your place one night. The aim is to make him see how fun it can be to play with a partner and to get him used to the idea. Promise your boyfriend you won't be mad if he takes all your money. Once he sees it's not weird for *him* to play with you, "drop him off" at poker a few times, lingering as long as you can. Be your affable, saucy self and drop a few subtle hints that you'd like to play. If you see other members of the game out socially, talk poker with them. Buy a round of beers. If you can get a few of the others in your camp, you're good as gold and will be buying in alongside your boyfriend in no time. In this case, it's good not to go *every* time (at least at first)—part of the allure of poker night is often that it's a night away from girlfriends, so you don't want him to panic that poker will never be the respite from relationships he craves.

WHERE TO GO GAME HUNTING

Hey, wait, you say. I don't even have a game to *get* into! How do I find one?

If there's no particular game you're interested in, but you want to start playing in home games—which you can expect to be mostly male—there are a number of ways to track down the species *pokerio playerus.*

Even if you don't live in a city, remember that with 60 million players in America, the odds are pretty good that you've got some near you. A few places to scout out games include the following.

✫The Office

If you work in a good-sized office, probability declares that there's a poker player in your midst—but who? You know how it's not hard to figure out that someone's going to therapy if she takes a two-hour lunch ever Wednesday at two? Well, if you've noticed Ken usually comes in dead tired the same day each week, he might be your man. Keep your earphones off and your ears open—if two guys in your office are in the same game, they'll be gossiping about it the next day. Once you've found your target, chat up cards while getting coffee, in the elevator, in the lunchroom, whenever, and finagle your way into becoming a poker buddy.

★ Cafés and Bars

Not only can you sometimes find postings or flyers for games in a coffee shop or bar, you can meet other poker players there, too. The week of the World Series, for instance, why not find a bar that's broadcasting the event and watch it there? You'd be surprised how often bars are showing the World Poker Tour and even Celebrity Poker on the televisions around the bar. Or bring this book or one of the other many poker books to a café and read it over a latte. Have a pen and paper handy so it looks like you're taking notes on it, even if you're not. If there's a poker player in the joint, getting his caffeine fix, don't be surprised if he asks you if you play or suggests another book. I've been asked by nonplayers as well—the national fascination with the game has never been higher and people in general are excited by the game and love to talk about it. Once you've found a guy, it may be as easy as exchanging e-mails until you're on way to his game.

★ Online

Shy? Don't work in an office or drink? Then you might try hunting around online for games. I don't mean virtually joining a boys' game over the Internet in an online casino, though that's also an option (see the next chapter). There are a lot of online message boards and meet-up groups just for poker players. Being that the majority of poker players are male, you'll most likely find games that are male-dominated. But there's no barrier to entry once you've found it—if someone posts a message that they're looking for players, they don't care about gender. They're looking to fill seats. If you're worried that they'll reject you if they figure out you're female, just use your initials instead of your full name. Because I have an asexual name, I've shown up for games that I've found through Friendster *(www.friendster.com)* or craigslist *(www.craigslist.org)* to find that they expected "Toby" to be a dude. But no one's ever looked disappointed when I show up, curves and all, instead. And many of the men I've met at those gatherings have become poker buddies who invite me around whenever they're playing.

All in all, playing in a boy's game is not inherently different from playing only with women. There's a different feel to the games—whenever the sexes mix, it adds a certain chemical charge—but the poker is the same, whether you play with your aunties or your uncles, your girlfriends or your boyfriends. Remember that as you riffle your chips and crack open a beer, and you'll do more than just fine.

GET YOUR HEART RACING FOR THE BOYS' GAME

BEFORE YOU HEAD OUT THE DOOR TO GAMBLE WITH THE GUYS, get revved up by listening to music not only about gambling, but also songs that make you feel like you're about to start out on an adventure, ready to jump on a motorcycle and kick doors open. Songs that make you want to strut. Take this list as a starting point and add whatever songs to the mix that will help you feel like the great goddess of gambling, ready to blow your opponents away on every level.

1. "Awesome"—Veruca Salt
2. "Big Spender"—Peggy Lee
3. "Boys Better Beware"—Dandy Warhols
4. "Cold Hard Bitch"—Jet
5. "Damn It Feels Good to Be a Gangsta"—Ghetto Boys
6. "Gambler"—Madonna
7. "Kish Kash"—Morcheeba
8. "The Lady Is a Tramp"—Frank Sinatra or Tony Bennett
9. "Money, That's What I Want"—Beatles

10. "Y Control"—Yeah Yeah Yeahs
11. "No Cheap Thrill"—Suzanne Vega
12. "Take the Money and Run"—Steve Miller Band
13. "Who's Got the Action?"—Dean Martin

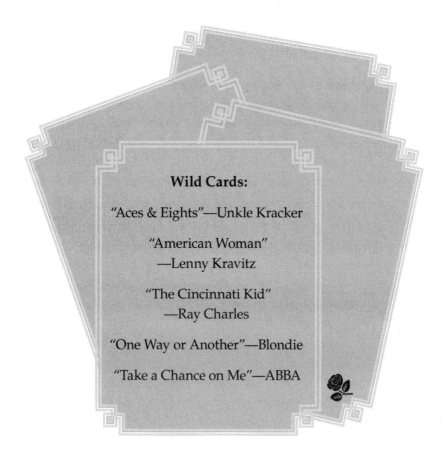

Wild Cards:

"Aces & Eights"—Unkle Kracker

"American Woman"
—Lenny Kravitz

"The Cincinnati Kid"
—Ray Charles

"One Way or Another"—Blondie

"Take a Chance on Me"—ABBA

OH WHAT A TANGLED WEB: PLAYING ONLINE

*My favorite thing about the Internet is that you get to go into
the private world of real creeps without having to smell them.*
—PENN JILLETTE

At first, I scoffed at Internet poker. The fun of the game is in playing in a room with real people. Where's the fun in playing online? Only lonely gambling addicts would bother! Besides, I thought, even if you get good at playing poker with other people on computers, there's no *way* that translates to playing against actual people. Right?

Sometimes a girl's gotta admit when she's totally, absolutely wrong. I was wrong when I thought stirrup pants, pastel paisley shirts, and puffy paint-covered sweatshirts were the epitome of style, and I was wrong about online poker. In 2003, Chris Moneymaker (yes, it's his real name) took $40, entered an online satellite tournament, and won a seat in the WSOP (full retail value: $10,000). He had never played in a brick-and-mortar, old-fashioned, people-filled tournament before, but he won it—to the tune of $2.5 million. Online poker sites exploded with hopefuls, yet I still doubted. It could be a fluke. But in 2004 the winner, Greg Raymer, once again had won his seat through an online satellite. He took home a mind-boggling $5 million.

I was clearly missing out on something—and no badass girl lets an opportunity slip past. Time for this moll to join the cyber-masses.

IT'S A WONDERFUL WORLD ... WIDE WEB

One of the things that can be offputting about playing poker online is the idea that you'll get confused by the software itself and lose money as you learn how to play. What fun is that? The people who run the sites are way ahead of you—at any site worth bothering to play at, they'll have tables where you use only "play" money. After downloading the site's software, you can start playing immediately and see how it works. You'll be able to get used to the action of online poker, see if you have any connection or speed problems, and decide how you like the interface and other players without ponying up one thin dime. You can quickly get a lot of practice playing one game, test out different strategies, and learn the ins and outs of new games without any financial risk.

In fact, as many as half of the tens of thousands of players on any given site are playing with funny money. That's right—tens of thousands on one site. If you wanted to put them all in the same place with tables and chairs, it'd more than fill a few football fields. Having the games online means that the only limitation to how many tables a site can run is not floor space but server space. It allows the online poker rooms to offer an immense variety of games at all sorts of different stakes, in both the play money and real money (or "live") games. You can start out small and play a 25-cent/50-cent game of limit hold'em, or you can pretend to be a high roller for a few hours and toss in a $300 raise in play money.

While half of the people on the site may be playing just for fun or to hone their skills, the other half manages to move an estimated $100 million in real money across online poker tables every night. And because the games aren't played in any particular state, but in the nebulous land of cyberspace (as of the writing of this), playing poker online is legal.

GETTING STARTED AND UP TO SPEED

The first thing you'll want to do is check out some of the online poker sites. The most popular and reputable ones are:

- **Paradise Poker.com** (*www.paradisepoker.com*)—This popular site has tournaments 24-7 and a reputation for having better players than other sites.
- **PartyPoker.com** (*www.partypoker.com*)—Currently the most trafficked site, PartyPoker.com has over 40,000 players populating its virtual tables at any given time. It is connected to the well-regarded **EmpirePoker** (*www.empirepoker.com*), but you can have separate accounts at each site.
- **PokerStars** (*www.pokerstars.com*)—This site is where both Moneymaker and Raymer won their entries to the WSOP.

It is one of the most heavily trafficked sites, with tons of tournaments and good customer service.

- **PokerRoom.com** (*www.pokerroom.com*)—This is the only place for Mac players, so it's my personal favorite simply on that basis. Windows and Mac users can all play not-so-nice together here. Ladies who Linux can come to the table, too.
- **UltimateBet.com** (*www.ultimatebet.com*)—This is where Phil Hellmuth, Annie Duke, and Russ Hamilton hang out online. If you can't get to a casino to lose a bunch of money to a legend, this is the place to try your hand against a great.

These sites are only a small sample of what's out there, and it doesn't really matter where you play as long as you check out the site first. Before you plunk down your real money or even sign up for an account at a site, you should do a little background checking.

SHOULD I PLAY OR SHOULD I GO NOW?

So you don't get into any trouble, find out the answers to these questions about any site where you're interested in playing:

1. **How do they keep your information and your money secure?** Even if you're only planning on playing in mock-money games, you'll usually still have to create an account and give your name, address, and e-mail. Make sure it's a secure site that won't sell your information, especially if

you plan on using your hard-earned cash. Check a site's FAQ section to find out what they're doing to ensure that your financial information won't be exposed or stolen. Also check to see what their policy is on transferring your winnings back to you.

2. **What's their customer service reputation?** Check the reviews for the site on the Rec.Gambling.Poker newsgroup and elsewhere (ask your personal research assistant, Mr. Google, for help) to see if complaints and problems have been dealt with quickly and pleasantly, or not at all. Since you're not in a brick-and-mortar card room where you can just wave your hand and get a floor manager to help you out, it's essential that a site's customer service be fast and reliable—you want to feel confident that you can reach someone, not just be shooting blanks into the vast void of the Internet.

3. **What do they do to prevent collusion (cheating) between the players?** Probably the biggest thing that keeps most people from playing online is the idea that online players are all in cahoots with each other—whether it's by instant messengering, having two computers side by side, or talking on the phone—as the game goes on. The best sites have elaborate software and programs to monitor betting patterns and kick out cheaters. Still, it is a real concern that there's only so much online sites can do about—but remember that there's collusion in brick-and-mortar card rooms as well. Just keep your eyes open.

⋆Click Here to Play

The first thing you need to do to get started playing is to download the software, which lets you play at the virtual games—which are colorful, animated places where avatars (computer-animated people) sit at virtual tables, complete with the sounds of chips and cards. Many rooms also have a chat feature that allows you to "talk" with other players in the game.

Both installing the software and learning to use it are made as simple (in most cases) as possible, so you can get started fast. Just follow the site's instructions. Once it's installed, you can choose what game you want to play in from the site's virtual queue area. You can see all the kinds of games that are going on and which ones have seats open. Pick, click, and choose how much of your real or virtual bankroll you want to sit down at the table with—and you're on your way.

⋆Who Is That Masked Woman?

There's one more thing before you start playing—you'll have to choose a username or handle that you're going to play with. You may also be able to choose what 3-D computer-animated kind of person (avatar) you want to represent your cyber-sassy-self.

Choose your name carefully—most likely, you won't be able to change it later. That doesn't mean you can't have fun with your name—or use it to deceive. You'll see a lot of people with names like *StansGotTheNutz*, *FlushDaddy*, *AcesNEights*, or *PokerManiac79*, but you don't have to choose a name that has to do with your real one, or even one that has to do with poker or badass girls. Use your "porn star" name (the name of your first pet plus the name of the street you grew up on), or become a favorite fictional character, or take on the trappings of a celebrity. You can give the impression you don't have a clue by including "newbie" in your name, pretend to be male by throwing an obviously male name in there, or you can leave them guessing with an asexual username. Of course, everyone knows this is possible and the other players may be trying to turn their title to their advantage as well. You can be anyone and be playing anyone online. There's even a Web site called Primate Poker (*www.primatepoker.com*), which purports that it has trained apes to play poker online and win. It could be true; the point is, you never know.

Therein lies the most important difference between playing in real life and playing online: it doesn't matter how old you are, what gender you are, or what you look like. No one can tell if you're sweating with nervousness, laughing with joy, or just picking your toenails. It also works the other way: you can't use body language or how people talk to read your opponents.

✫Can You "Tell" Anything Online?

Obviously, you can't pick up on how that fellow taps his lips when he wants to raise, or how that woman flushes when she bluffs, but there are a few ways you can gauge your opponents. This only really applies in real-money games, since in funny money games, people play extremely loosely and fold much, much less often, since it's not costing them anything and it's more fun to play the game than to wait to play the next hand.

Some people watch timing—but this isn't always a good indicator since hesitation may just be a slow Internet connection, while a fast response may just be someone using an "auto call" button. But you can watch the size of your opponents bets and try to notice betting patterns. Some people will always play when they're in a certain position, be it big blind or button, while others will always raise the same amount when they have a pair.

There are things you might want to jot down as you play— you can make a little table to fill in as you play each game to make it easy. You might include:

1. How often does a player fold, and when (preflop, flop, turn, river) and why (didn't want to call, was reraised)?
2. Are there any positions a player almost always stays in on (the blinds, on the button)?
3. Do they usually flat-call or raise if they stay in a hand?
4. Do they ever check-raise?
5. If you're playing no-limit or pot-limit, take note of the size of their bets and raises. Do they always make the same opening bet? Are they fond of doubling the pot?

Keeping a log like this is good practice and keeps you from getting bored and just IM-ing "a little" as you play. It's also a good way to start learning how to keep notes on players in your real games— even if you don't bring a pen and paper and do it in your head.

BADASS BREAKDOWN: PROS AND CONS

There are advantages and disadvantages to playing online, depending on what kind of player you are. Me, I'm easily distracted while online, checking e-mail, IM-ing friends, surfing the Web. None of this makes me a good online player. Just as you shouldn't do your nails or start chatting on your cell phone at a real poker table, the same goes for online poker. On the other hand, it serves me well in that I can play a lot of hands very quickly, try out new tactics free or very cheap, and I can just sit in a few hands anytime I want, even for just twenty minutes.

If you're still on the fence, I'll break down the pros and cons to help you decide:

☆Advantages

- You are a faceless, genderless, unknown player.
- You can practice your game at most rooms with "play" money.
- It's nonintimidating and easy to start playing.
- You can play whenever you want, for as long as you want.
- There are always a variety of games to play, at a variety of stakes.
- If you have a lot of physical tells, no one will know.
- You can do things like take notes and use a calculator while playing and no one will bother you about it.
- It can help you start thinking less about money in actual terms and more as one of the tools of the game.
- The software makes sure no one plays out of turn, reminds you when it's your turn and what your options are, and even tells you when you're making an incorrect play such as folding when you can simply check.

⋆ Disadvantages

- You can't use reading people to your advantage since there's no body language to judge.
- You need a fast Internet connection for most sites.
- While it's carefully monitored, it is possible for people to work as a team and cheat using chat software, phones, and other methods.
- It's easy to spend way too much time in online card rooms.

SPECIAL CONSIDERATIONS WHEN THE MONEY MATTERS

There are particular positives and negatives when you're playing online with your dough, including the following:

- Because of the large volume of players and low overhead—no dealers or rent to pay—the rake in online casinos can be a smaller percentage. It's kind of like a discount warehouse of poker—think Costco or Sam's Club. You don't get the selection or the more high-end products, but you get a good deal. The point is, a lower rake means you get to keep more of the money you win.
- There's also no dealer or waitresses to tip.
- Currently, almost all of the online poker rooms have "sign-up bonuses" and other promotions—many give you a 20 to 25 percent return up to $100 just for putting real money in an account. Others give you bonus money if you get a friend to sign up—and sometimes your friend gets a bonus, too.

- Without actual, real chips to play with, it's easy to forget you're playing for real money, and you can end up losing more than you meant to.
- A large percentage of the people you'll be playing with will be amateurs, so what and how they play is unpredictable.
- On the other hand, more amateurs may equal more money for you.

Whether you're a computer geek or prefer to use the Internet only to e-mail your friends, there's no denying that playing online is perhaps the easiest and most inexpensive way to get a lot of experience playing poker in the shortest amount of time. Every day, more and more people are playing poker online, and I expect that we'll be seeing even more of them in the flesh at the big tournaments in the years to come.

SECTION THREE

BEYOND LADY LUCK

Serious poker is no more about gambling
than rock climbing is about taking risks.

—A. ALVAREZ

PLAYING THE DUMB BLOND: USING BEING FEMALE TO YOUR ADVANTAGE

I don't mind living in a man's world
as long as I can be a woman in it.

—MARILYN MONROE

The fact of the matter is, if you're a woman and you're sitting down at a game for the first time, most men are going to assume you're probably not a good player. Women, too, for that matter, are more inclined to believe that they're better than an unknown woman than an unknown man.

Some men don't believe women have the skills to bluff or play deceptively. Kathy Liebert, one of the best pros playing today, has noticed that "often if a woman checks the man will assume she is weak and will bet. If a woman bets or raises they will often give her credit for a good hand."

So men think we're stupid and honest. The question is, How can you use this bias to your advantage and win more money?

NO TRUTH IN ADVERTISING

There's a principle behind most advertising campaigns that goes by the acronym, FUD. It stands for fear, uncertainty, and doubt, and it's how they get you to buy that antiwrinkle moisturizer and sweet-smelling deodorant. They show you a beautiful woman who looks in the mirror to discover that, uh-oh, she's got crow's feet! Or she's standing next to a good-lookin' fella, smiling away, only to have him sniff the air, make a disgusted face, and walk away. *Oh no!* you think—do I have crow's feet? Do I smell? Maybe it's my smelly, wrinkled self that's the problem. If I were just less lined and odoriferous, my life would be better.

Well, there's something called advertising in poker, too. And it's used for the same effect. In poker, when you show your hand unnecessarily—for instance, if you're in a showdown and you're already beat—you don't have to reveal what you played with. But if you do, you're advertising, and usually what you're trying to sell is that you're a terrible, loose player. Why would you do such a thing?

Here's the trick of it: If people at the table believe you don't know what you're doing and are likely to stay in a hand with unsuited rags just to "try your luck" or throw money after long-shot draws, they'll be more likely to call any bet you make. So when you do have the best hand, more people will have stayed in with you and you'll win more money. For a long time in my regular Thursday night game, everyone thought of me as someone who bluffed a lot, because I would always show the hands I shouldn't have been playing in the first place. The truth is, I'm not that big a bluffer, but I made a lot more money on the hands I won than did other players who were perceived as rocks. It took a long time before the boys shifted their idea of what kind of fish I was.

There are times when advertising yourself as a loose player isn't a great idea—for example, if you're at a game with a lot of calling stations, you're going to get your bets called by a lot of people anyway. Your best bet in that group might be to show a really premium hand that you folded, like a pair of queens, to advertise that you're a really tight player so those calling stations at least think twice about seeing your raises. So watch the action in the game you're into decide how best to portray your poker ability.

SIX POKER PERSONAS TO PUT ON

Just as advertisers cater their campaigns to the demographics, it's good to tailor your table image to the game you're playing. And just as marketing mavens try out different tactics to see which is most effective, you should test out a variety of characters to see which ones work for you and in what situations.

It's also just plain fun to play a part for an evening—if you know the game you're going to will be a one-night-poker stand, you can act however you want and don't have to worry that it'll ruin your reputation. When joining a game you plan on going to regularly, however, it's probably smart not to act too outrageously or put on a persona that will be hard to remove—the effort of keeping up your image may make the game less fun. It's kind of like wearing overelaborate undergarments on a night when you just want your date to rip off your clothes and get to bed—by the time you're through with the bells and whistles, you're too exhausted to enjoy the fruits of your labor.

✴The Dumb Blond

As Amarillo Slim once said, "It never hurts for potential opponents to think you're more than a little stupid and can hardly count all the money in your hip pocket, much less hold on to it." This works best in new games. Pretend you've never played poker—if that's too far a stretch add "outside my family's annual Thanksgiving game" or just pretend not to know the particular games they play. Misread your own hand as often as possible—declare you've got "three of a kind and a pair" instead of saying you have a full house, or if you miss your flush, exclaim with joy that you've got four hearts as you show your cards. Midway through a hand, ask what three in a row beats.

Signature Move: Repeatedly "forgetting" what color chips stand for what amounts and throwing the wrong number of chips into the pot.

Signature Saying: "I just can't keep track of what beats what."

Pros: Since no one will believe you know what you're doing, they'll stay in more pots with you, try to bluff you out of hands more, and never guess that you're slow-playing that nut flush in your hand.

Cons: Hard to bluff or intimidate anyone out of the pot. Not great for our collective badass girls poker image.

✸ The Flirty Minx

Dressed in your lowest-cut blouse, a skirt slit up the side, and heels, walk into the game and turn on the charm. Let your bra straps show. Declare your best game is really strip poker. While you're thinking, "absently" touch your lips, your throat. You know how to work it. All I'm saying is, when a man gets distracted, he doesn't play as well. Additionally, it may lead to some good leads for dates.

Signature Style: If it's boobtastic, it's fantastic. Red lipstick, strappy stilettos, mini-skirts.

Signature Saying: "I bet you're hiding something big in that pocket."

Pros: Besides the general distraction attraction, if you can get a guy interested in you, he's less likely to play aggressively against you. He may stay in pots with you just to keep interacting with you across the felt, in hopes he can parlay that into interacting with you outside the game.

Cons: If you're not interested in the guys but they become smitten with you, it can get awkward over time—like it did in high school when you flirted your way into borrowing that science homework from the gawky guy who then proceeded to follow you around the halls for the rest of the year.

✸ Just One of the Guys

You're playing with the boys, so why not act and dress like one? Wear your butchest outfit—paint-covered overalls with a white muscle tank underneath, a man's suit, wear a baseball cap—whatever makes you feel kinda manly and will fit in with whatever the men are wearing. If someone lights a cigar, ask for a puff. Swear as you talk about the bad beat your home team just suffered. Tell the dirtiest joke you know and invite them to tell a more tasteless one.

Signature Move: Showing up with a six-pack, guzzling one down, and letting out a big belch.

Signature Saying: "Did you catch the game last night?"

Pros: Great for getting yourself accepted as one of the gang at the boys' game.

Cons: Not necessarily great for getting yourself dates out of those boys.

☆Cold, Hard Bitch

PMS anyone? Comedian Roseanne once said "Women complain about premenstrual syndrome, but I think of it as the only time of the month that I can be myself." If you can relate, then this one's for you. Revel in being a bitch. Smirk as you pull in pots—gloat. Yell when you suffer a bad beat. Think Heather Locklear's Amanda on *Melrose Place,* Sharon Stone in *Basic Instinct,* Joan Collins on *Dynasty,* Sarah Michelle Gellar's character in *Cruel Intentions.* Be ruthless.

Signature Move: The aggressive reraise and the sneaky check-raise; you're going to make them pay for it.

Signature Saying: "You are going to be so sorry you messed with me."

Pros: People will be afraid to enter pots with you. They know if you're in a hand, it's going to be expensive. They'll expect a check-raise anytime you check and may let you get a free card.

Cons: If you don't hit your hand, all that raising can get expensive. If you scare people too much, no one will call your bets and the pots you win will be smaller. Plus, people may get pissed off at you.

Caution: If you're in a regular game, you can't pull this one even once a month if you want to be invited back. Unlike your boyfriend, these guys don't have to just get used to your monthly mood swings.

☆ Party Girl

Sometimes at a party, you pretend to be drunker than you are so you can flirt more and "accidentally" bump into a certain someone. You can say a few forward things to get a guy's attention and announce your interest—things you would *never* say if you were sober—with the ready excuse if your advances fall flat that you didn't know *what* you were doing because you were just so drunk. Take that attitude to the table. Say you came straight from happy hour as you hand over not quite the right amount of money for the buy-in. Make sure you get a cocktail before you sit down. You don't have to drink it—think of it as an accessory. If you can slur or have a wardrobe malfunction, all the better. Be a drunken distraction.

Signature Moves: Clumsily knocking over your chips. Losing interest in the action and never betting until someone is forced to remind you it's your turn.

Signature Saying: "Anyone want to do a shot with me?"

Pros: Since you're "drunk," people will think you'll make poorer decisions and play looser, and they are more likely to stay in hands with you all the way to the showdown.

Cons: Sometimes pretending to be drunk ends up with you actually getting drunk, making you play looser and make poor decisions.

✮ Girl Next Door

Gosh darn it, you just hate to win against her cause she's so . . . *nice*! She's always saying please and thank you and asking if she can get anyone anything from the fridge when she gets up, and look at her—with her hair in a ponytail and her white tennis shoes. The object is to be thought of as a kid sister, that all-around nice girl they grew up with. Works best if you already know a few of the fellows and can ask them questions about their families, pets, or other friendly neighbor topics. Befriend strangers by earnestly requesting their advice on strategy and complimenting them on their wins.

Signature Move: Bringing homemade chocolate chip cookies and a 2-liter of soda.

Signature Style: Jeans and a white T-shirt, flower-printed dresses. Freckles.

Pros: If the guys believe you're just too nice to lie—you don't have it in you—they'll give you credit for whatever it is you're holding. If you check, they'll assume weakness; if you bet with that aw-shucks blushing smile on your face, they'll fold.

Cons: All that smiling hurts.

✮ Secretive Sphinx

A stone-faced mystery. The kind of girl who's a riddle wrapped in an enigma cloaked in a devastating black Dolce & Gabbana dress. React as little as possible to the cards or other players and rarely talk. No matter how much other players beg, never show or talk about the hands you fold. Be ritualistic about every aspect of your play—look at your cards exactly the same way every time, count to ten before making your move, be it bet or fold. Smile only while you stack your racks.

Signature Style: Large, dark sunglasses, hats with veils.

Signature Saying: "I guess you'll never know."

Pros: Being unreadable is one of the skills most pros aspire to. Besides the obvious advantage eliminating your tells will give your game, you'll frustrate other players as they try to figure you out. They'll be more likely to call your bets all the way to the end just to get a peek at your precious cards.

Cons: Difficult to maintain through a whole evening, especially if cocktails are involved. It's also not the most "fun" way to play and isn't conducive to making friends.

Still can't decide which poker personality is most your style? Don't think you can pull off anything but your good old self? You don't have to be a diva of deception to just play up your natural tendencies. Discover what kind of table image to try by taking the quiz in the extra-credit section at the end of this chapter.

WINNING THE BATTLE OF THE SEXES

Whether or not you choose to use a façade to enhance your feminine advantage, if you're winning, you may still benefit from one male flaw: Some men just can't stand to be beaten by a woman.

Silly as it seems, a lot of men relate their "manliness" to how they do at the table—it *is* kind of emasculating to get schooled at the poker table. Luckily for us girls, we don't have to worry about that nonsense. But if you see a fella fuming about the fact that you—*you* of all people!—have most of what used to be his stack in front of you, he's probably going to start staying in more pots with you, calling every bet you make, hoping he can win some of his pride and money back from you.

Knowing that, you can wait until you have a great hand and raise freely, knowing he'll keep calling, throwing his money to lil' ol' you. Just a woman. Who wins.

1. Driving alone, your tire blows out. What do you do?
   a. Pull out the jack and the spare and get to work
   b. Calmly call AAA and wait patiently
   c. Pose by the side of the road to entice men to stop and help
   d. Cry uncontrollably, then get out and kick the offending tire

2. If you had your pick, you would spend Halloween:
   a. Handing out candy to neighborhood kids
   b. At a masquerade
   c. At a party, dressed as Marilyn Monroe or Britney Spears
   d. Not eating all the chocolate before the kids arrive

3. If you were a beverage, you'd be:
   a. Domestic beer
   b. A dry martini
   c. Champagne
   d. A boiler-maker

4. When you get really excited . . .
   a. Your hands shake and your heart races
   b. You'd never know
   c. Hmm? Excited how?
   d. Everyone within a fifty-foot radius knows

5. If a guy you're dating makes you angry, you . . .
   a. Get him back with a prank
   b. Give him the silent treatment
   c. Make sure he sees you flirting with another guy
   d. Get drunk and leave belligerent voice mails for him

6. If you could have a superpower you'd choose:
   a. Flight
   b. Invisibility
   c. Is being superhot a power?
   d. To control the weather

7. If you were a shoe, you'd be . . .
   a. Loafers
   b. Sneakers
   c. Heels
   d. Lodged so far up your ass for asking such a dumb
      question

✭Badass Broad Scoreboard

Count up how many of each letter you picked and see what you have the most of. If you're all over the place, you've got the potential to portray them all, you chameleon you.

If you picked mostly a's

Your casual, comfortable style and positive, can-do attitude make you a natural for Girl Next Door or Just One of the Guys.

If you picked mostly b's

Keep to yourself much? Quiet, sneaky, and able to control your emotions, you're a Secretive Sphinx.

If you picked mostly c's

The Flirty Minx or the Dumb Blond will suit your natural tendencies to use your feminine charms to your advantage.

If you picked mostly d's

When you're happy and you know it, clap your hands, Party Girl. But mornings when you roll out on the wrong side of the bed, it'll be a Cold Hard Bitch of a day.

PLAY THE MAN, NOT THE CARDS: BLUFFING AND READING PEOPLE

Yeah, well, sometimes nothin' can be a real cool hand.
—*COOL HAND LUKE,* 1967

ack when I played with my parents at our house, the last hand of the night was always Indian poker. In Indian poker, each player is dealt one card, face down. You don't look at your card, though. That would ruin the fun. What we'd do next is lick the back of the card and smack it onto our foreheads, so everyone *else* could see the card. (If you're playing, you don't have to lick it, you can just hold it up with one hand, but where's the fun in that?)

In Indian poker, you bet on whether or not you think you have the best (highest) card, based on the cards you see stuck to everyone else's foreheads and what you can tell from each person's face as they look at your card and the other players. Do they seem happy while they look around the table? Do they look longer at you than others at the table? It's a highly silly game, but it provided an early, uncomplicated beginning to the idea that you could tell a lot from a person's behavior at the table. An expression of "jeez" or a quick intake of breath could mean someone sees a lot of aces—if you look around and don't see any other high cards, you can bet you've got the ace. Since it was the last game of the evening, I'd also have a good idea about what kind of people I was playing with—whether they liked to bluff, if raises made them fold, or if at this point in the long evening they were going to call anything at all. With all that in mind, I could look around the foreheads of my opponents and decide if I was the high chief of Indian poker—or at least if I could convince everyone else at the table I was and get them to fold.

Learning how to get a feel for what kind of players you're sitting with and observing any telltale signs they have that indicate what they're holding is one of the most crucial skills to becoming a better poker player.

WHO ARE THE PEOPLE IN YOUR NEIGHBORHOOD?

Before you start worrying about just what it means when Bill pushes back his glasses before he bets or Jill flips her hair after looking at her cards, you'll want to identify what style of poker each person is playing.

★Loose vs. Tight

A loose player (like the proverbial loose woman) plays a lot of hands. Loose players want to see every flop, be part of every pot—they're impatient and just want a lot of action. A tight player is the opposite—she waits for premium hands and good opportunities to enter pots.

✮Passive vs. Aggressive

Passive players tend not to raise, but only check and call. Many passive players are of the mindset that they're saving money by betting conservatively, and they will fold to big raises. If they raise, you can be sure they have a strong hand. Aggressive players, on the other hand, are more likely to raise than call. If they do check, they may be waiting to check-raise. They figure if you want to play with them, it's going to cost you.

Once you can determine how to characterize the characters in your game, you'll be a lot more informed about what your best move is against them. If there are a lot of loose, passive players—also known as "calling stations"—you know they'll be a lot of people in every hand and it will be difficult to try and muscle everyone out by raising. If you've pegged a guy as a tight, passive player—also known as a "rock"—any time he enters a hand, you can bet that he's got a strong hand and if you don't, you can fold. If you've got a "maniac"—or a loose, aggressive player—in your midst, you know to watch your back. Maniacs will bet and raise with anything or nothing at all. They love to get more money in the pot and fake people out of hands. Last is the challenge of the lot, the tight, aggressive player. These are the pros of the game—it's the ideal way to play poker. They don't play a ton of hands, but they mix up their play enough so you don't know just by their bet, check, or raise what they have. Sometimes they bluff, but it seems more often they don't—and usually they're the winners at the table in the long run. The tight, aggressive players are the ones who've read the books and know the odds, so you know to be wary of them, but if you know the strategy they're following, you can still try to predict what they're holding.

It's also good to notice if a player shifts from one kind of behavior to another in certain situations. After a few drinks, many people become looser players (yours truly included), or more aggressive in their bets. Others will always start out playing tight and aggressive, but become freer and easier with what hands they play as the hours roll on. Or a loose player might shift to a more conservative betting pattern after a few big losses. The more you can notice, the more of an advantage you'll have. If you can shift your style to suit the players in the pot with you on any given hand, you'll be rewarded for your correct play—in the form of huge piles of chips.

READING THE SIGNS: TELLS

One of the funniest things I've noticed about watching the actors on Bravo's Celebrity Poker is how bad some of the actors are at deceiving their opponents and hiding their hands. Hams at heart, they overact enormously, rolling their eyes and sighing too loudly to feign disinterest in their strong hands, belligerently staring and goading their opponents to call their bluffs. This kind of acting, on TV or in your home game, is the easiest tell to spot. If you know your fellow players, you can usually tell when they're overcompensating for a bad hand or trying to pretend they've got a miserable hand so you'll call their nut straight.

The best way to start learning tells is to pick one player a night to watch, like he's the only show on television. Watch his face when he looks at his hole cards, when the flop comes. Notice when he bets and raises. Does he call a lot? How did he behave when he held that full house? What was different about his play when he was trying to bluff you out of a hand? Does he glance at his chips when he's going to bet? If you can answer even a few of these questions and remember the answers, you'll find that you start winning more hands and folding more losers against him.

You'll pick up most of that through familiarity and using your female intuition, but there are a few involuntary and common tells that you can watch for even the first time you sit down with someone.

If a player . . .

Acts uninterested: If a gal acts like she's not interested in what's happening in the hand and starts casually chatting up opponents, looking around the room, watching TV, and almost studiously avoids glancing back at the action, she's probably trying to hide a really good hand.

Is anxious and fidgety: If the action hasn't come to Sir Shakes-His-Leg-a-Lot, this may indicate that he's eager to bet his good hand. Alternately, if he's already bet and is watching the betting move around like it's the last leg of the Kentucky Derby, galloping toward a knuckle-biting finish, he's probably hoping no one will bet. He may have a drawing hand or one that could be drawn out on, but he's nervous about too many people calling his bet.

Checks her hole cards after a flop: If in a community card game, the flop shows the possibility of giving someone a flush or straight and you see a player rechecking her hole cards, she's probably checking to see if she has a card that fits the flop. She doesn't have the flush or straight already—when you've got two spades in the hole and the flop comes all spades, you know you've got the flush without looking. But if you see someone recheck her hole cards and take a long time to decide before calling, she's probably calculating odds for a straight or flush draw to see if it's worth her while.

Has shaking hands: This one's the most common. If you notice someone's hands are shaking as he places his bet, boy, oh boy does he have a hand. The myth is that people's hands shake when they're nervous about a bluff, but in reality, when a guy's hands start really trembling, it's because he's so excited about his hand he just can't contain himself, hard as he may try.

Stares at everyone: In life a direct gaze is a challenge, and it's true in poker, too. Only in poker, usually it's to cover a bluff. It's akin to animals who puff themselves up to try to fool predators into thinking they're bigger and more dangerous than they actually are—but it's all air and noise. If you're being stared at in an "I dare you" fashion, take the dare if you've got a hand.

SOMETHING FOR NOTHING: BLUFFING

If you couldn't win sometimes without having the best hand, poker wouldn't be any fun at all. Bluffing is part of the legend of poker, of tales of outsmarting unsuspecting opponents out of killer pots and winning hands with nothing more than cheek. But in reality, there's a lot less bluffing in poker than rumor would have you believe. One of the common mistakes that rookies make is believing they *must* bluff a certain amount to play poker. Of course this isn't true—it would be better never to bluff at all than to bluff just for the sake of doing it. You might bluff to advertise, as we discussed earlier, but that's for a real purpose, not simply to check some "I bluffed this hour" box in your poker checklist.

In most games, you won't be playing at high enough stakes to ensure that you can really muscle every single person out of every pot just by raising the maximum. Knowing this, most players won't just raise and raise with absolutely nothing just for fun. Instead, good players pick their opportunities carefully. Overall, bluffing works best when there's only one or two people left in the hand. Makes sense—easier to outwit one person than a whole team.

Good times to bluff are when:

- You sense opponents have weak hands.
- You're last to act and feel that a bet will cause most people to fold.
- There's a strong hand possible on the board and you don't feel anyone has hit it.
- You're on a draw that has a good chance of improving.

The first three are the most obvious—you come on strong because your gut is telling you that no one has anything worth defending. Any bet will cause them to fold. In the case of the third, you're going to try and represent that you've hit a flush, or that the ace that came on the river was just what you were waiting for. You're trying to scare them out of the pot, using the frightening board cards to tell your ghost story.

The last one is not a typical bluff but something known as a "semibluff,' and it is in the toolbox of most good poker players. For instance, let's say you are playing hold'em, and after the flop you've got four cards to a flush or straight. You bet, hoping that people fold, but knowing it's still possible for you to end up with a really good hand on either fourth or fifth street. When you bet on the flop, you're technically bluffing, since you don't have a hand at that moment, but you're betting on the possibilities for your hand and trying to make it expensive for others to gamble on the chance that you don't have a hand and won't get the cards that would help you.

Just remember, bluffing is an important tool to use along with reading people, but if you think it's a good idea to bluff anytime, anywhere, the only thing you'll be doing is fooling yourself out of a pile of cash.

IF YOU REALLY WANT TO LEARN ABOUT THE MEN YOU'RE BATTLING at the baize, use this to keep track of the guys you plan on seeing regularly in games. You don't have to fill in everything—or keep an accurate count how many hands everyone entered; just filling in "a lot" or "few" is good enough to get a basic idea of what kind of poker player someone is.

It also works for keeping logs of online players and female foes, though obviously you can't check out a guy's looks or if he's wearing a wedding ring online.

Name: _____

Favorite Game: _____

Single? _____ If so, cute? _____

Gut feeling: great, good, fair, or poor player? _____

Poker Personality:

[ ] Calling station [ ] Rock [ ] Aggressive

[ ] Loosey Goosey   [ ] Bluff Baron

Tells? _____

Strengths and Weaknesses: _____

Memorable Moves and Moments: _____

_____

_____

Game-by-Game Breakdown:

Date/Time/Place _____

Played _____ hands*   Won/Lost $ _____

_____

Date/Time/Place _____

Played _____ hands   Won/Lost $ _____

_____

Date/Time/Place _____

Played _____ hands   Won/Lost $ _____

_____

Date/Time/Place _____

Played _____ hands   Won/Lost $ _____

_____

Date/Time/Place _____

Played _____ hands   Won/Lost $ _____

_____

Date/Time/Place _____

Played _____ hands   Won/Lost $ _____

_____

*You don't have to count exactly how many hands, "few" or "loads of" is enough.

YOU CAN NEVER BE TOO RICH: IMPROVING YOUR GAME

*If a man has one hundred dollars and you
leave him with two dollars, that's subtraction.*

—MAE WEST

No one's perfect. My mother may disagree, but I know I have flaws. Life is filled with unpleasant surprises—from ruining another white shirt to hearing your ex-boyfriend is asking the next girl to move in with him—and we fool ourselves. We say it doesn't matter that the coffee will never come out of our brand-new blouse, and we joke that rubbish living with trash is so fitting—as we toss back our heads in an insouciant laugh. We're so witty, so urbane, so over the pittances of life! But it does affect us. And you've got to admit that to yourself if you want things to improve.

Now that we've got *that* out of the way, here are a few basic things you can do to vastly improve your hold'em game.

HAVE THE TITS TO FOLD

Probably the number one thing most players can do to improve their game is to fold more, both before the first round of betting and after. It's hard to stay out of hands, especially if you haven't been getting dealt good cards for a long stretch. Soon enough, really marginal hands like K-3 unsuited and Q-7 suited seem pretty good. In fact, they seem great! But you've got to learn self-discipline. Just as we know we must deny ourselves every beautiful pair of $500 Jimmy Choos we set our eyes on—as darling as they are—we must also learn not to enter every pot. And once you're in a hand, there are times you have to learn to let go.

⋆Letting Go of Hands

Don't get attached to those aces. Hands like A-K are particularly hard to let go of—they had so much possibility! You had such hope for that perfect flop! It's like getting a blue box from Tiffany's—could it be . . . ? But it turns out just to be a box your boyfriend had lying around from when he got a key chain for Christmas that he used to put some junky novelty watch in to give you. That ain't right. And you'd know to get rid of a guy who played with your hopes, right? Just as you recognize the right thing to do would be to fold that fellow, if the cold, hard light of the flop turns your pocket cards from treasure to trash, don't pretend it's still worth something. Put it in the trash pile and let them take it away.

✮Letting Go of the Blinds

A common mistake many players make is that if they are the big or little blind, even if there's a lot of preflop raising, they won't fold—even if they've got a terrible hand. This is especially true with the big blind.

The thought is that you already have your money in the pot, so you may as well call and stay in for the flop. But you shouldn't be thinking of the blinds as a bet you've already made—that money is gone, your once-a-round fee for playing. Remember also if you're the big or little blind, you are in the two worst positions. After the flop comes, you'll be the first or second to act.

So if someone raises, consider if you would call or raise that bet if you weren't the big blind—or if you even would have stayed in the hand in the first place. If you wouldn't, in most circumstances, you should muck your hand and save yourself a bet you can use when it'll really do you some good.

✮Dames Don't Tilt

No one likes losing, especially when you expect to win. When this happens more than once in a row in a game, it's common for players to lose their heads and play badly. It's called "going on tilt"—a term that comes from pinball machines. Knock one a little, that's okay; it's part of the game. Bump it a bit too hard, and you get a warning. But when you hip-check the machine for all your worth in order to jolt that silver ball from its doomed path straight down the center, you cause the machine to tilt. Whether or not that ball moved, it's gone. Not only is your turn over, the machine takes back any bonus points coming to you at the end of the ball, so in fact, you've done worse than you would have had you just let it go.

To put it in a real-gal context: When you wake up one morning and snag your last pair of hose on the day of your big presentation, it's annoying. But you're cool, you take it in stride—you've got time to stop in at the store on your way to work. When you hit traffic, your patience wears a little more. But it's not until just after you triumphantly pull out of the Kmart and onto the road, new hose at your side, and some guy rear-ends you that you really lose it. And no matter how hard you try, you can't shake that feeling. You're distracted by what you'd like to do to that guy's rear end as you talk your way through what should have been a promotion-worthy presentation. It happens to the best of us—it's human nature.

Players tend to tilt more, and worse, when they lose big hands, but the tilt seesaw goes both ways. Some players tilt when they win as well. They play looser, stay in more pots, and call and raise against the odds. That's how I am—I'm fine when I lose, but when I win, I turn into a maniac. I tilt so hard the balls crack the glass. And when I win two in a row? Fuggitaboutit. When I pull in two big hands in a row, it's like something in me short-circuits. My hands shake like crazy. I flush. It starts the moment I know I'm going to win pot number two, and it's a terrible tell.

The best advice I can give you about tilting is to watch yourself and figure out when and how you tilt. Notice I didn't say "if"— because there's going to be something or someone that's going to get your goat. It might not be winning or losing—it could be teasing from another player that makes you feel you have to "prove something" by staying in a hand.

Once you've figured out how and why you tilt, you can figure out what you need to do to bring yourself back to level. For instance, unless I get dealt bullets on the next hand after a big win, I fold it. I know my urge is just to "play one more"—whether I get dealt Big Slick or 2-7, I feel "lucky" enough to justify staying in. Meanwhile, I'm spending so much energy trying to take deep breaths and calm myself, I hardly notice what is going on in the game. Who bet? Did someone raise? I have no idea. I get frantic again when the action returns to me, trying to catch up. It's a bad cycle, and I've tossed away half of what I've just won before I regain control. So I force myself to fold. There's no right way to prevent tilting, but start with deep breathing and any other means you would use in ordinary life to stop yourself from going ballistic or exploding into tears.

USE YOUR HEAD

The more you play poker, the more you'll hear people throwing around terms like "pot odds" and "outs." You don't have to be a statistics wizard to use the numbers of the game to your advantage. It can be complicated and there are those who can tell you precisely the odds of hitting an inside straight on the river without blinking an eye, and furthermore exactly how much money has to be in the pot already to justify whatever bet he's considering making. In fact, the difference between the advantage of a player like Mr. Math over someone who learns the basics of odds and outs is a lot smaller than the difference between someone who knows the basic odds and a new player without any idea.

What I'm saying is that it is worth your while to try tackling the statistics side of the game, but don't worry about knowing everything to the last decimal point.

✮ Know Your Escape Routes

In Texas hold'em, once you've seen the flop, you'll have to decide whether or not to stay in the hand. If you've already made your hand—lucky you, there's no need to calculate anything other than how to extract the most money from your opponents. But the majority of flops won't be that simple. You might have three cards to a flush, four to a straight, or a pair you're hoping turns into trips. What are the odds of that happening? One way to gauge that decision is by figuring out how many "outs" you have—that is, how many cards left in the deck can improve your hand if they show up on the turn or the river. Since the only cards you know for sure have been dealt are the cards you're holding and the cards you see on the board, you assume that all the cards you need are still available. In other words, don't worry about guessing what other people have when you're counting up your outs.

For example, if you're holding:

A ♣ Q ♣

And the flop comes:

Q ♥ 10 ♣ 2 ♣

You have a lot of outs. How many? Well, any club will help you. There are nine unseen clubs (thirteen, minus the two in your hand and minus the two on the board), which would give you a flush; there are two queens left, which would give you trips, and there are three aces left, which would give you two pair. Altogether, that gives you fourteen outs, which is a lot.

On the other hand, if you were holding:

7♦ 7♥

You would have very few outs at this point. You can't make a flush or a straight, and the only two cards left to help you are the pair of sevens left in the deck. Not great. But if the pot is big enough, it may be worth your while to stay in.

✭ Stirring the Pot Odds

This is where a lot of people get their heads spun around by the math, but I'm going to keep it as simple as possible. The basic idea behind pot odds is that you want enough money in the pot to make it worth your while to take a chance and bet on your hand. The more of a long shot your hand is—say those two 7s—the more money has to be in the pot to make it a good bet. On the other hand, if you had that A-Q of clubs, you'd need far less money in the pot to justify a bet.

To calculate the pot odds you're getting, just add up the money in the pot and compare it to how much you have to bet. You don't have to be precise—just guesstimate. If, for instance, it looks like there's about $50 in the pot and it's $5 to stay in, you're getting 10 to 1 odds on your money. If you have better than 10 to 1 odds of improving your hand, you should stay in. If it's worse, fold.

How do you figure out the odds of improving? You've figured out how many outs you have, and you know there are (after the flop) forty-seven unseen cards. So in the first case, there are fourteen cards that will help your hand and thirty-three that won't, which equals 14 to 33 odds (14/33). Since you have two chances of getting those outs, you add each chance up (14/33 + 14/33), so you discover that you have 28 to 33 odds of getting your hand, which is roughly even. In other words, there's an equal chance you'll hit your hand or won't every time.

While it's good to know how to calculate the odds, even a math moll like me finds it easier just to memorize what the odds are for the most common situations and go from there.

After the flop, if you have . . .	Common Hand	Odds
2 outs	hoping a pair becomes trips	11 to 1
4 outs	inside straight draw	5 to 1
8 outs	open-ended straight	2 to 1
9 outs	flush draw	2 to 1
15 outs	flush and straight draw	1 to 1

The key one to remember is that once you get to eight or nine outs, you're getting 2 to 1 odds, so there only needs to be $2 in the pot to make betting $1 worthwhile. With thirteen, fourteen, or fifteen outs you're getting even odds and any bet is a good one, odds-wise. If you've got more outs than that, you're golden.

So, if you're following, you can see that those pair of 7s may be worth betting after all if there's $50 in the pot and the bet is $5.

That's 10 to 1 odds for an 11 to 1 shot. And if you expect anyone to bet after you, you might get exactly the right odds after all. If the pot were $20 and the bet was $5, it wouldn't be worth the risk, but with the right amount of money, it's worth it to take the chance.

LOCATION, LOCATION, LOCATION: USING YOUR POSITION

In poker, like everything else, timing is everything. The deal rotates around the table not only so the blinds rotate, but also because of your position. Just as in real estate, there are desirable locations to reside in and not-so-great areas.

The best position is last position: the dealer. The dealer is the last to act in every round of betting after the flop, and therefore she has the most information to use to make decisions about betting, raising, and folding. It's just like how it's better to have time to Google a blind date and maybe call some mutual friends for some dirt before the date; you'd rather know who's in the hand with you, how many people are involved, and if they're coming out raising. The more information you have, the better decisions you can make.

You've got to adjust your play to the position you're in. If you're in early position (one to three seats to the left of the dealer), play more conservatively with better hands. In middle position, you can loosen up a little, while if you're seated in late position (the dealer or the two to her right), you can afford to play sketchier hands, since you already know how many people you'll be up against and what it's going to cost you.

Late position is also a prime spot for stealing pots. When the bet is checked all the way around to you and you're the dealer, often making any bet at all will cause everyone else to fold. You may be in for a check-raise, but if this ploy works one time out of two, it'll be well worth your while.

Once you've got these skills in your utility belt, you'll start seeing your winnings increase each night, and, before you know it, you'll be researching implied odds and effective odds and rattling off facts and figures at the poker table you didn't even know you knew. Believe me, I hadn't realized how much of this stuff I had committed to memory until I was in a game and a new player asked the table, "Who knows what the odds of being dealt a pocket pair are?" and before most others could even register the question, I had blurted out "16 to 1." It's not really a useful fact to know, but it did earn me a lot of respect from the table.

If you want to improve even more, I highly recommend picking up one of the dozens of books that focuses solely on hold'em and furthering your education in what has become my favorite kind of poker.

THE SKY'S THE LIMIT: PLAYING IN CASINOS

Now look, mister, the first rule of the game of poker, whether you're playing eastern or western rules, or the kind they play at the North Pole, is put up or shut up!

—DENNIS WILCOX IN *A BIG HAND FOR A LITTLE LADY*

laying poker in a casino can be intimidating at first. Compared to the inviting main floors of casinos, sparkling and vibrating with noise and light, the bells and whistles of slot machines suggesting easy money and entertainment, a casino's poker room seems almost businesslike. There are no flashing lights, no soundtrack of music or coins cascading onto each other, and these days, more often than not, you can't smoke. But that's not to say there isn't a lot going on.

The first time I went to the Trump Taj Mahal in Atlantic City, even though the gracious poker room manager gave me the grand tour, the room overwhelmed me. The room seemed the size of a football field, packed with tables and players, the cacophony of noise echoing that of the boardwalk outside, the whisk of cards against the felt and the clay chips clacking against one another like the sound of the waves breaking and receding over the sand on the beaches outside. Above that, there was the din of players making small talk—*Where are you from? How often do you play?* and *Just can't catch a hand*—between calling and raising and the moans of the second-best. Add to that the dealers directing the action, declaring winners, the floor managers announcing the initials of players like barkers over speakers, and the concession call of waitresses, "Cocktails? Cocktails, anyone?"

It's hard to take it all in and know what to do. But there's no reason to worry. You know the rules of poker, now you just have to learn a variation in the game.

If you're really concerned, many hotels and poker rooms offer free lessons for beginners. They'll go over the basics of the game, but you'll get a chance to sit at a table—so you can get your butt groove in the chair on and really get comfortable.

STEP-BY-STEP TO STEPPING UP TO THE TABLE

I can't be by your side the day you first step into a card room, but here's a woman-to-woman walkthrough.

☆Step 1: Get in Line

Before you sit down in a casino game, you're going to have to get on the queue for the game. At most rooms, there's a clear place where the poker room host, or "brush," takes names and watches the room—he's sort of like a maitre d' or host at a restaurant and usually has a podium or desk much like in a restaurant. The bigger the room, the bigger this front desk area will be. There may be a whiteboard or, in some of the newer card rooms, an electronic bulletin board that lists the games and the initials of the players who are waiting to get into each game. If you're not sure where to go, just ask a waitress or anyone wearing a nametag. To be a badass about it, toss her a buck nonchalantly as you strut to the desk. Plus, if she's working your area later, you'll get better service all night.

When you put your name on the list for games, the person in charge might ask you what games you "want up" for—which waiting lists you want to put your name on. There are usually a variety of games going on, and it's normal to ask what the options are, or what they "spread." (When a new game is started, they may announce they are about to spread that game: "We're spreading 3/6 Hold'em.")

With more and more poker room newbies, card room employees are used to helping novices understand what different abbreviations mean and explaining things in plain English.

You still may encounter lists and charts that look like secret code, but it's pretty easy to decipher the meaning if you look over the list of abbreviations in the following table.

No-Limit Hold'em	NLH	NL Hold'em
Limit Hold'em	LHE	Hold'em
Pot-Limit Hold'em	PLH	PL Hold'em
Pot-Limit Omaha (high)	PLO	PL Omaha
Omaha Hi-Lo 8	O/H/L/8	Omaha/8 or Omaha H/L
Seven-Card Hi-Lo 8	7S/8	stud/8

The limits in fixed-limit games will be displayed as well as 2/4, 3/6, 5/10, 30/60, etc. So a listing for a fixed-limit hold'em game with the limits of $4 and $8 would be 4/8 hold'em. Just like when you put your name on the list at a restaurant, it's okay to ask how many people are in front of you and how long it might be. Just as a hostess can only guess how long a party will linger over coffee and cocktails, it'll be an estimate—and it's harder to guess how many hours someone can last playing cards than how long it will take someone to milk those last drops of wine. It's a good idea to put your name on at least two or three lists. Be prepared to wait—especially for the more popular lower-limit games. On a recent weekend trip I took to the Borgata in Atlantic City, one player reported a four-hour wait for the $2/$4 tables. On the other hand, another guy got a seat in a $6/$12 hold'em game in thirty minutes.

When your name or initials are called, go back to the podium to find out where your seat is. You can keep your name on the lists for the other games—and it's not a bad idea, since you may decide you want to try a different table for a variety of reasons. There might be another game you were more interested in playing, you may not like the people at the table where you're sitting, or you might be angling for whatever game a certain someone who's caught your eye is playing at.

★ Step 2: Get Some Chips

Once you've been told what table you'll be at, you'll need to "buy in" to the game—some places you buy chips at a cage, others at the table from a floor person or chip attendant. You can usually also buy from the dealer at your table, but since it slows down the action, if there's another way, try that first.

How many chips should you get? At a limit game, get at least ten times the amount of the higher limit. If you're playing at a 3/6 game, $100, or "a rack" of chips, is a good amount. You can always buy more chips, but there's no harm in having a lot of chips by your side.

Once you've ordered your chips, you can start playing, even before the chips arrive. It's called "playing behind." The dealer may ask you if you want to post a big blind to start playing right away. I recommend holding off until your chips arrive and the big blind reaches you. That way, you can spend a few hands calming your nerves and checking out the competition.

☆Step 3: Get Ready for Action

The first thing you'll notice is that the game goes much faster than a home game. At a home game, you might see ten to fifteen hands an hour, while at a casino you could play thirty to forty hands. That's why the dealer's there—it's his or her job is to keep the action going. You might notice that instead of simply shuffling the cards the mythical seven times that's supposed to be the perfect shuffle, sometimes the dealer just messes the cards about on the table before pushing them back together and shuffling a few times. That's normal—again, it's a faster way to shuffle and therefore shortens the time between hands.

Additionally, there's less small talk in general around the table—you don't know each other and you're not going to become friends. While you probably will talk to the people sitting to your right and left, it's not the kind of atmosphere where you get so engrossed in a conversation that you lose track of the game—and if you do, the dealer will remind you it's your turn.

The dealer is not just a taskmaster; he is also a resource. If it's your first time in a card room, there's no shame in telling the dealer and asking him to explain any aspect of the game.

When the big blind reaches you, you'll post your first bet and, voilà—you're playing in a card room. Believe me, breaking that seal is a lot less painful than some others, if you know what I mean. And this first time will probably be a lot more fun.

WHEN IN ROME . . . CASINO CUSTOMS

You've already mastered the essential etiquette, and from Caesar's Palace to New York, New York, you'll be considered a picture-perfect player if you follow the guidelines in Chapter 3. The most important things to remember in a card room are:

- Remember to make sure you say "raise" if that's what you're doing.
- When you fold, make sure it's obvious and that you push your cards close enough to the dealer that he or she can reach them.
- Casino card games are always played with table stakes—meaning that you can only play with the money you have in front of you at the beginning of a hand. If you are running out of chips, place a bill under your stack to indicate you want to buy in for that amount, and if you do run out of chips, you will still be able to bet against that money.

- When you win a pot, you are *expected* to tip (or toke) the dealer. Like waitresses, most of dealers' income is from gratuities. Rule of thumb: Tip the small blind bet if you win a normal pot, the big blind if it's a big pot. If it's a monster, just be generous.
- The drinks may be free, but you should still tip the waitresses for each one.

THE FINE PRINT

Unlike every other game in a casino, poker is not a game of players against the casino, but players against players. The house isn't in the hand. So how does the casino make money? With something called a "rake" (or "vig")—a percentage of each pot (usually around 5 percent of the whole pot) that the house keeps as a fee for letting you use their tables.

Instead of taking a percentage of each pot, some card rooms have you cough up a set fee each time the dealer changes, or they set an hourly rate that the dealer will collect for the house. They'll collect it on the hour, and it's usually the amount of the big blind at your table. Rules and rates of the rakes are usually posted somewhere pretty easy to find. Don't be a guy and refuse to ask where to find the information—the difference between a 3 percent rake and a 7 percent rake will make a huge difference in your pocket at the end of the night.

The rake is why the dealer is paid to keep the action moving—more hands equal more money for the casino, and because the dealer makes money from tips, he's motivated.

Your first reaction might be, *Well, why should I pay anything? I don't pay to play at home.* Well, you don't pay your mom when you go home for dinner, but you're not at home now. It's the simple difference between eating at home and eating out—you're paying for service and atmosphere, and a level of experience you can't create at home, no matter how fancy your poker room becomes. Just think of it as paying for those "free" vodka tonics and the stories you'll get to bring home to the girls at your regular game.

TAKING BREAKS AND CALLING IT A NIGHT

There are no commercial breaks or intermissions in a card game in a casino, so if you need to take a bathroom break, satisfy a nic fit, or just get a breath of fresh air, wait until you've folded a hand and tell the dealer to deal you out until you get back. You don't have to take your chips with you—they're safe on the table.

While you're gone, if you miss the blinds, you'll come back to a token or reminder from the dealer that you'll need to post your blinds to come back into the game. (You can also wait until the blind comes back around to you.)

If you're plain done with poker, most people quit right before the big blind reaches them. Announce that you're done, stand up, and "rack up" or "color up" your chips to take over to the cashier to collect your winnings.

Like playing online, you can play for as long or as short a time as you like. There's another player waiting to take your place. And another seat waiting for you another time—and since many poker rooms are open 24-7, that can be anytime you fancy.

SPARKLY DIAMOND SONGS FOR CASINO CRUISING

FLYING INTO VEGAS, ITS SUDDEN BRILLIANT SPARKLE IN THE middle of the dark desert, is enough in and of itself to quicken your pulse. The only thing that could make it better is having "Viva Las Vegas" playing as your soar over the landscape of signs—it makes you feel like a movie star, part of the ongoing adventures that Vegas is famous for. Driving up to Atlantic City, Foxwoods, Tahoe—it doesn't matter what man-made paradise of lights you pull up to—the right music will make it all the better.

1. "Ace in the Hole"—Bobby Darin
2. "Atlantic City, My Old Friend"—Robert Goulet
3. "Casino Queen"—Wilco
4. "The Card Cheat"—The Clash
5. "Do It 'til You're Satisfied"—B.T. Express
6. "Easy Money"—Billy Joel
7. "Have a Lucky Day"—Morphine
8. "Lets Go to Vegas"—Faith Hill
9. "A Little Less Conversation"—Junkie XL remix of Elvis Presley

10. "Money"—Pink Floyd
11. "Telling the Dice How to Roll"—Patrick Tuzzolino
12. "Viva Las Vegas"—Elvis Presley (ZZ Top cover works, too)
13. "Your Love Is Like Las Vegas"—The Thrills

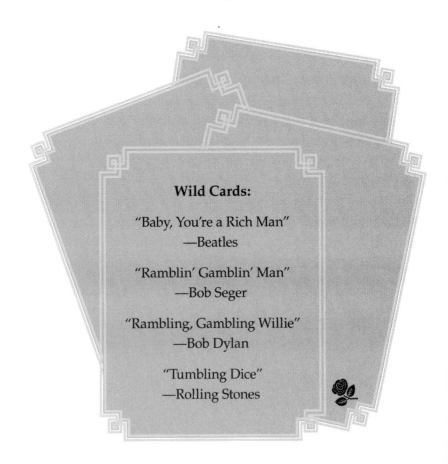

Wild Cards:

"Baby, You're a Rich Man"
—Beatles

"Ramblin' Gamblin' Man"
—Bob Seger

"Rambling, Gambling Willie"
—Bob Dylan

"Tumbling Dice"
—Rolling Stones

WELL-STACKED AND BUSTING OUT:
PLAYING IN TOURNAMENTS

Limit poker is a science, but no-limit is an art. In limit, you are shooting at a target. In no-limit, the target comes alive and shoots back at you.

—CRANDALL ADDINGTON

Playing in a live tournament is exciting. It's a winner-takes-all battle, a contest where luck and skill combine, and to win it all, at some point you're going to have to risk losing it all. It's a chance to put yourself in the shoes of the pros you've seen on TV—and if you've got the cash, you can even play against them.

You don't have to fork over $10,000 to enter the World Series of Poker to play in a poker tournament (remember, Chris Moneymaker and Greg Raymer both won their entries online). The first no-limit Texas hold'em tournament I played in was just one table, held in a coffee shop on the Upper West Side after hours. The ten of us handed over $60 for a seat at the table. I came in fourth, which was one out of the money, meaning I left with nothing but a memory of a good time.

Most poker tournaments are no-limit—it's sort of a game that prefers winner-takes-all. There are limit tournaments and ones that combine the two games—say the first hour is limit hold'em and the rest of the tournament is no-limit. To simplify things, I'm going to stick to no-limit tournaments, since those make up the lion's share of the action.

PLAYING WITH FUNNY MONEY FOR REAL

In the World Series and World Poker Tour tournaments, players in the main event are playing with chips that do represent the actual amount of money being gambled with, but in most tournaments, this isn't the case. You see, in no-limit tournaments, chips have no real value as money—they're only valuable as a tool to use against your opponents. Once you've paid your buy-in, or entry fee, the only way you're going to see that money again is to survive long enough to "place"—and how much money you get is determined by how long you can last. You can't decide to stop playing and keep what you've got; everyone's in it together until the end.

Instead of playing with regular casino chips, you'll get special tournament chips—just to prevent anyone from getting the bright idea to pocket a $10,000 chip for later. There are a number of reasons that you play with funny money, but the best is that there's something thrilling about pushing around such large amounts of money—raising hundreds, thousands, tens of thousands of dollars on a single hand.

Another reason is that in tournaments, the blinds don't stay the same amount all night long, but creep up at each level. But before I get into levels and rounds, you need to know what kind of tournament you're entering.

Even within no-limit, there are a few variations you should know.

Tournaments like the World Series of Poker are "freeze out" tournaments, which simply means that everyone buys in with the same exact amount of chips and no one can get more during the tournament. People keep playing until they run out of chips, and the one who ends up with all the chips is the winner.

On the other hand, many tournaments allow "rebuys" during the course of a tournament. What this means is that during a fixed period of time—usually the first hour of play—if players bust out completely or their stack dwindles below a certain amount, they can pony up some more potatoes and buy more chips.

There also may be an opportunity for players to "add on" a certain amount to their chips at the end of a certain time period, regardless of the size of their stacks. So let's say you enter a tournament in which $30 starts you out with 1,500 in chips. The "add on" might be a chance to buy another 1,500 in chips for another $30.

Finally, there are certain tournaments that are called "satellites." A satellite is simply a tournament where the prize is entry into another tournament. That's how Moneymaker and Raymer did it; they won online satellites for seats in the WSOP.

LEVELS AND ROUNDS

The only real difference in the way the betting and stakes are handled in a tournament as opposed to in a real-money, or "live," game is that in tournaments the limits increase as the night continues. When you buy in to the tournament, they might tell you it will have twenty-minute levels—this means that every twenty minutes, the limits (and therefore blinds) will increase. Rounds or levels can be as short as fifteen minutes or as long as an hour, but they'll remain constant throughout the tourney, and at the end of each level, the blinds will usually double.

Additionally, in some larger tournaments, after a certain level, an ante on top of the blinds may be added to each hand.

THE CHIP RACE

After certain rounds, players will be asked to trade in their lower-denomination chips for higher denominations. It makes sense—when the limits are $1,000/$2,000, you don't really need to hold on to those $50 chips you started with. Counting them all up just slows things down.

If you end up with a few chips left over after you've traded up all you can, you'll be part of a "chip race" with all the other players who have leftover chips. Everyone puts their odd chips in front of them, and the dealer gives you one card, face up, for each chip—it's like getting one raffle ticket per chip—and the winner (or winners, depending) are decided by who has the highest card.

WHO'S IN THE MONEY?

The last thing that's unique to most tournaments is that there is not just one winner, but a "prize pool." There are tournaments where the winner truly does take all, but in most tournaments, cash prizes are awarded to at least the top three (or final three) players, and in most cases, many more than that. If you manage to make it and win part of that prize pool, you have "cashed" or landed "in the money" in the tournament. As soon as they've gathered all the money and crunched the numbers, someone running the tournament will announce how many people will place in the money, and will usually bring out a chart displaying how much each spot pays.

By the way, when the stakes are high, gamblers sometimes leave off the zeros when they announce their bets. Instead of raising $500, they'll say it's "a nickel." So, $1,000 becomes "a dime," and $10,000 is "a big dime."

Now that all that business is behind us, we can get to the badass business of playing in a real-live, good old fashioned, no-limit tournament.

BADASS NO-LIMIT TOURNAMENT TIPS

It would take an entire book (and there are many out there) to adequately teach tournament strategy. Knowing the strategies outlined in the beginning of this section is the best preparation, but no-limit tournament play has quirks and quandaries unique to the wild animal it is. So these are just a babe's basics—enough to get a gal going.

⭐Tip #1: Be Aggressive! B-E Aggressive! B-e A-g-g-r-e-s-s-i-v-e—Aggressive!

If your usual style of poker is more passive than aggressive, it's time to switch gears. Aggressive already? Time to ramp it into high gear. In tournaments, people will try to steal your blinds, come over the top and try to raise you out of pots, and generally muscle you around. You have to do the same—if you play too conservatively, your chip count will go down and down and you may end up getting "blinded to death"—meaning you have to use most of your stack just to post the blinds.

⭐Tip #2: Let Them Fight Amongst Themselves

While aggression is key, this does not mean you have to play like a lone gunslinger, knocking out every opponent one by one. Especially in the middle rounds of a tournament, let the other players knock out one another and fight your battles for you as much as possible.

⭐Tip #3 Draws Are the Kiss of Death

While in limit poker it's often worth it to stay in to try and hit a flush or straight—after all, it's just one more bet—in no-limit, it'll probably be far too expensive to pay to see one more card, and if you don't make your hand, you'll have thrown away a lot of chips. Unless you've also already got a high pair to back up your draw, especially in the later stages of tournaments, let go of draws if someone bets into you heavily.

☆Tip #4: Watch the Stacks

Pay attention to who's got big stacks and who's short-stacked at the table and where you stand. You should always be trying to build your chip count, but be aware of which players you're going up against. Players with bigger stacks than you may go all-in to get you to do the same, while smaller-stacked opponents are good targets for you to force into going all-in if you've got a strong hand. In general, when extremely short-stacked players go all-in, especially on the blinds, it is often an act of desperation—they figure they don't have enough money to last through another round of blinds, so they'll push all-in on hands like K-10 and A-9, thinking it's now or never.

Meanwhile, if you hold the big stack at the table, it's easy to start playing loose—you've got chips to throw around! But don't start playing recklessly and risk chips just because you can—you're not there yet. You can afford to be choosy with the battles you enter, so make it count and make your stacks last. You'd be surprised how fast a big stack can be halved through loose play.

☆Tip #5: Always Remember "All In" Can Equal "All Out"

Remember that every time you go all-in you have to win the pot or it's over. Be careful of going all-in when you don't have to—even if you've already got a lot of money in the pot. Even if you've already bet 10,000 of your 40,000 in chips on your ace-10 suited and someone comes over the top and goes all-in, you might consider folding. You don't have anything but an ace-high and if your opponent has even a small pair, they're already a favorite to win. It's not the time to gamble—keep the 30K and use it to bring that guy down when you have the nuts.

✰Tip #6: Adjust Your Play to the Stage of the Game

Just as you change tactics and techniques from the beginning of a relationship to when you're officially dating to when you're hoping to move in together, you've got to adjust your game to the action of the tournament.

Early in the tournament, especially if there are rebuys, most people play looser. You can afford to take risks if you're willing to come up with the cash to buy more chips. Plus, since the blinds are still pretty low, you can afford to try and hit a few draws. If it's a freeze-out, or the rebuy period is over, in general you should play tight. Don't go all-in unless you're pretty damn sure you have the best hand. You don't have to get everybody's chips right away. But you do have to keep at least a few chips longer than the others. Survival is key.

Halfway through, once the field has been narrowed substantially—halved, at least—but there are still a good number to go until everyone left is in the money, it's good to open up and play more aggressively. The closer you get to the prize pool, the more your remaining competitors will tighten, hoping to at least last long enough to cash. It's a good spot to steal blinds.

One of the sweetest moments in a tournament for those still playing comes after the worst moment for another: the player who gets knocked out "one off the money," meaning that at that stage all the remaining players are in the money, and will get a piece of the prize pool. You feel her pain but you're so glad it wasn't you.

Once you've reached a stage where everyone playing is in the money, in general, players loosen up a little and start taking more chances. Players figure they've at least gotten their money back and can afford to take risks and be more aggressive. So tighten up again and let them have a field day eliminating themselves, saving you the trouble.

This continues until it's down to the final twelve or so players and everyone again tightens up, hoping to last until the final table. Again, it's a good time to play aggressively, because people are so concerned with lasting that they won't call unless they have premium cards.

When you reach the *final table*, you'll see fewer and fewer flops and multiway hands—usually at the last table most hands will end up head to head. Look around and try to figure out if anyone's still just trying to last (as opposed to those who are determined to win). The players who are just hoping to hang on as long as possible are good targets for you to focus on and steal pots. As each player gets eliminated, you can loosen up your requirements for starting hands—with only three or four people, any ace becomes worth giving it a shot, even low pairs are strong, and more than ever, you have to be able to read your opponents. At the final table, it's easy to second-guess your gut, but listen to it—you've been playing for hours with these guys and your instincts are probably smarter than your card-addled head. It's not just your badass brain that's gotten you this far, but your heart as well, and if you can listen to what each has to say, you very well may walk away a winner.

DEALMAKING AT THE FINAL TABLE

If you're lucky and skilled enough to last until the final table, and you last until there's only three or four players, you may find the other players discussing "making a deal" before the tournament ends to split up the money differently than the official payouts. For instance, let's say the payouts are $6,000 for first place, $2,000 for second, and $1,000 for third. But instead, the final three players agree that no matter who wins, the first place contestant will get $5,000 and the second and third will get $2,500 apiece. Whether you decide to do this is up to you—if you're the short-stacked one at the table or the least skilled, it may be the safest bet. Some pros and casinos frown on dealmaking, feeling that it corrupts the game.

Now you're ready to take that pink Cadillac of poker out for a spin. Don't worry if it ends up a total wreck your first time out—it's a tricky ride, but it sure is thrilling. And soon enough you'll be shifting gears and handling it like a pro, with a smile on your face as you ride off into the sunset with a suitcase full of money.

SECTION FOUR

GAMBLING WITH ALL YOUR HEART

Poker is a lot like sex, everyone thinks they are the best, but most don't have a clue what they are doing!

—DUTCH BOYD

LUCKY AT CARDS, LUCKY AT LOVE: MEETING MEN THROUGH POKER

That beats the lot. A woman who can pick out a grade-A cucumber and knows a thing or two about poker. Where have you been all my life?
—BIG LOUIE IN *THE PERFECT PLAY*, BY LOUISE WENER

Although I had just gotten out of a four-and-a-half year relationship, I didn't start playing poker regularly to meet men—it was just part of my "have more fun" plan. I had been wanting to join my best friend's husband's game for months and months, and as a single gal, I had nothing to stop me from putting aside Thursdays to play. I did want to get out and date and have fun, though, and, being hetero, it wasn't like my all-female book club was crowded with possibilities.

WHY THE TABLE IS A GREAT PLACE TO MEET MEN

More and more at parties, I found myself talking about the last World Series of Poker or places to play in the city. I got invited to other games around town, which led to other games—and at each one I sat down at a table full of possibilities beyond what cards I'd be dealt and what I would do with them. It seemed there were virtually thousands of young, interesting, single men playing poker on any given night in this city. I realized I was on to something:

Good odds–It's a fact: more men than women play poker. The first time I followed the popular advice columnist idea of taking a class that appeals to men more than women, I signed up for a martial arts classes at a Dojo that was 90 percent male. Unfortunately, instead of the grounded Zen studs I hoped to meet, that school had overly aggressive, macho types. Plus, you don't have to play poker in oh-so-flattering sweat pants. Most home games are dominated by guys, and the casino card rooms are usually filled with a wide sea of men sprinkled with a handful of women.

Few wedding rings–Because poker is the kind of game played at night and well into the wee hours, there aren't a lot of family men who can get away with staying out drinking and gambling—at least not more than once a week. Girlfriends and wives tend to cut down a man's poker time, too (unless he's lucky enough to date another poker player . . .).

Something to talk about–Unlike meeting a blind date or trying to pick up someone in a bar, you don't have to come up with pickup lines or excuses to talk. You're all there first to play poker, so there's no pressure to go through the routine of small talk and getting-to-know-one-another questions. There are no awkward silences you feel the need to fill with chatter—you've got cards to look at, people to watch, bets to consider, and, of course, other people to talk to. Conversation is always easier when you have something in common, and poker players love to talk about the game as much as I like to relate every detail of how I got the deal of the century on a dress.

Great atmosphere–Wherever you're playing, the mood is energized—there's money at stake, people holding their breath as they wait to see if the next card is the one they're hoping for—and whichever way the card turns, they exhale out words. Bad beat or fantastic win, it takes no effort to commiserate or congratulate. And it's easy to tease as you raise and flash a coy smile when you call. Flirting goes with poker like ice cream goes with pie—both are good on their own, but much more delicious together.

Low-pressure setup–If you are in a regular game, it can be a low-key, pleasant way to get to know someone over a number of weeks. Unlike a party, where you've got one shot to make your impression and hope that hottie asks for your number, the guys in your regular game aren't going anywhere; if it doesn't happen this week, no big deal—the next week holds another opportunity for suggesting a nightcap after the game. Or suggesting that you hit a different game together some night.

The 4-1-1–My favorite thing about meeting men to date through poker is that you can learn a lot about what kind of man someone is by what kind of player he is. Very rarely will a guy modify his table image or behavior because a woman sits down— he's busy using that energy to keep cool in the face of aces and bluff people out of pots. So if you watch how he acts and talks at the table, it's like getting an advanced peek at what you'd be getting into without having to spend weeks learning date by date.

What can you tell about a man at the poker table, other than his card-playing ability? A man who doesn't respect you at the poker table won't respect you at the dinner table. And his style of play may tell you a lot about him:

If he . . .	He's probably the kind of boyfriend who . . .
Gets mad when you win pots off him	Expects to always get his way and would prefer that his girl-friends were always slightly less accomplished than he is
Takes you seriously as an opponent	Would treat you as an equal in a relationship
Goes a little easy on you (especially before he has time to see what a badass you are)	Has a sweet and chivalrous side
Doesn't mind losing money to you	Picks up the check at dinner
Is passive, easily raised out of pots	Is somewhat insecure, as unsure of himself as his cards
Doesn't toke the dealer or waitress	Is a cheapskate
Is very conservative in his play	Likes schedules and order and predictability
Has a short temper over a bad beat	Has a short temper about every-thing else, too

With some men, the first night at the table you'll see the kind of emotional displays you'd normally only see two months into a relationship. It'll save you lots of time. And as we girls know, it's always better to have more information before you have to make a decision.

MEETING MEN OUTSIDE THE TABLE

When my fiancé and I split, I signed up for an online personals service. In my profile, my answer to the question "If I could be anywhere at the moment, I'd be . . ." was "Playing poker until 2 a.m. and winning." I added "Texas Hold'em" to my list of interests. As I sorted through the responses online, I noticed that more often than not, it wasn't my picture or my witty response to "Most Humbling Moment" that caught guys' attention, but the fact that I liked poker. Additionally, those men tended to be the ones I was most interested in. Of the men I actually met in person, more than half played poker regularly and most of the good dates were with card-playing chaps.

It's easy to talk shop with another player. And, in addition to having fun, I got some good recommendations for books, heard about different games, and was invited to attend a semiregular game. Over the past year, I've struck up conversations with strangers about poker in bookstores, with coworkers at lunch, in elevators, even on the subway—you'd be amazed how often the opportunity to chat up cards comes around.

With the popularity of poker at an all-time high, it's ten to one that at least one of the guys you're checking out at a party or a bar plays poker. It's also a good bet that you'll pique his interest if you reveal that you play. You get instant credit for being a little daring, a sassy, independent broad, one who's not afraid to play with the big boys and take a risk. There's just something about a girl who plays cards, I've been told.

And badass that you are, you'll soon be shuffling more dates than you can count—I recommend investing in one of those day planners. Odds are you'll need it.

DON'T MUCK IT UP: POKER DATING DO'S AND DON'TS

Worm: "I guess the saying's true. In the poker game of life, women are the rake, man. They are the fuckin' rake."

Mike McDermott: "What the fuck are you talking about? What saying?"

Worm: "I don't know. . . . There oughta be one though."

—*ROUNDERS*

hether you decide to take home a fellow as well as a tournament prize or set your sights on a stud in one of your regular games, dating another poker player comes with its own set of rules and regulations. Of course, you won't get thrown out of the dating game for breaking these rules, but if you follow these tips, you'll stack the deck in your favor for fun and romance.

DO . . .

Set up the house rules—I don't mean whose house you prefer to end up in (though that's not a bad idea, either), but laying out your expectations. While within the game of poker, deception is allowed and a good idea, if you're about to start dating a guy who you already see regularly at poker, be straight about what you want out of it. You're already involved in one game with this guy—try not to add romantic game-playing to the mix. If nothing else, be clear about if and how this will affect your regular poker game.

Stay out of multiway pots—If there's another girl or two at the game who are clearly vying for the same guy, deal yourself out. Unless you're a clear winner and he's a jackpot worth risking female friendship and messing up the game, avoid the trap of going for a guy just because everyone else is doing it.

Leave the cards on the table—If you are dating a guy in the game, don't gloat if you win more, or get mad if he wins a large pot off of you. That's the game, and you shouldn't expect him to go easy on you, or vice versa, just because you're involved outside of the table.

Go head to head—One of the perks of playing poker with someone is the playfulness of it, the sparring across the table. Enjoy it. As Angelina Stark put it, "talk about sexual energy. I've never been so turned on as when I first played a guy I was dating heads-up. Remember, the family that plays together, stays together."

Use what you know—There is nothing shameful about using a tell you've learned in another setting at the poker table. Maybe, because of a recent rendezvous, you know he holds his breath when he's really excited; if you see him peek at his cards and not exhale, you can use that to your advantage and fold. No one else has to know how exactly you knew he had pocket aces.

Settle up at the end of the night—If you are in the midst of a spat or want to have a heart to heart, the table is not the time or place to battle it out. Once the cards have been put away and you two are on your own, you can talk his ear off, but making snide comments or barbed asides is a losing way to play both the game of poker and the game of love.

DON'T...

Be afraid to start the action—You should have learned by now that sometimes aggression is the only way to win. Making the first move is a bold, badass move that every girl should try, and any guy worth pursuing will respond to it.

Show your cards—Be discreet about dating other players at the table. Don't demand to sit next to your sweetie or shower him with public displays of affection. It's a sure way to make your beau and the others uncomfortable, and may lead to the suggestion that you two come on separate nights.

Play more than one hand at a time—One player to a hand is a good rule for the table, too; you can date as many people as you like, but dating more than one guy you run into at the same table isn't a smart move. At least at the same time—though if you space it out enough, it might be okay. Just remember: guys gossip, too.

Play the man, not the cards—Sometimes its more tempting to enter pots with the current crush, or stay out of ones with your raising Romeo. Play your paramour as you would anyone else, as hard as it may be. It'll make you a better player overall if you can separate your emotions from the game.

Expect him to leave with you—If you play in a game with a guy you're dating and you're through for the evening, don't expect him to get up and go with you, especially if he's winning. Unless you've made definite plans to leave together, don't count on it. If you were on a lucky winning streak, you might not want to get up and leave to get lucky either.

DIG A SPADE DEEP INTO THE GAMBLING BLUES

SOMETIMES YOU'RE DOWN ON YOUR LUCK. THE BOY YOU BET ON turned out to be a bad play, or lay, or just took off with all your lingerie. At the felt, it's all bad beats and dirty rags—nights of cards running colder than my ex's heart. And let me tell you, that's awful cold. It gets to a gal.

Dive into the pit of despair, have a good solid wallow in the melancholy mud, and come out when you've washed off the muck with a good cry. Listen to the blues and relate. It's kind of badass.

1. "Blackjack"—Ray Charles
2. "Dying Gambler's Blues"—Bessie Smith
3. "Gambling Blues"—Eric Clapton
4. "Gambling Polka Dot Blues"—Jimmie Rodgers
5. "Gambling Woman"—Chris Thomas King
6. "Heaven or Las Vegas"—Cocteau Twins
7. "Leaving Las Vegas"—Sheryl Crow
8. "Little Queen of Spades"—Eric Clapton
9. "Losing Hand"—Ray Charles

10. "Luck of the Draw"—Bonnie Raitt
11. "Lucky and Unhappy"—AIR
12. "Ooh Las Vegas"—Cowboy Junkies
13. "Shape of My Heart"—Sting

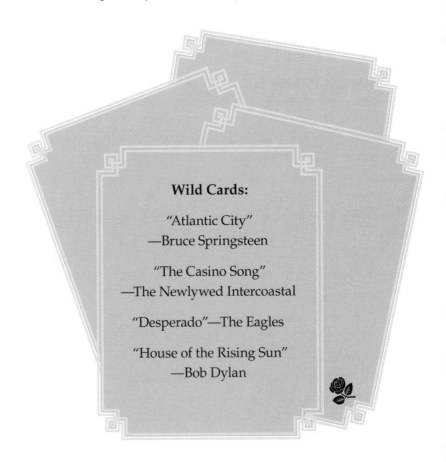

Wild Cards:

"Atlantic City"
—Bruce Springsteen

"The Casino Song"
—The Newlywed Intercoastal

"Desperado"—The Eagles

"House of the Rising Sun"
—Bob Dylan

QUEEN OF HEARTS: IMPROVED RELATIONSHIPS THROUGH POKER

Most human beings conduct their lives as a series of risks, some more calculated than others. They may not like to admit it, especially to themselves, but they bluff their way through life's complexities, both professional and personal, every day.

—ANTHONY HOLDEN, BIG DEAL

I've often wished I had started playing poker seriously earlier in my life. It would have saved me a whole lot of heartache. The more I've learned about the game, and gotten into the habit of making good decisions in play, the more I see how one can apply the principles of poker to matters of the heart.

KNOW WHEN TO FOLD

I firmly believe that had I started learning the theory of poker earlier, I wouldn't have stayed with the wrong man as long as I did.

At the beginning of the game I thought I had been dealt an incredible hand—the hand of my dreams—a royal straight flush of hearts.

So I bet on that hand, strongly and completely. I invested time and effort—and one quality I always had in spades was patience.

But as more cards were revealed, and my hand was coming up with nothing, I refused to see it. I clung to even the slimmest chance that it would work out—or else, I thought, I would have wasted all that time. I thought I could just wait it out, play the hand I was dealt while I waited for the unbeatable hand—the wedding band on my finger. It would all be worth it, I thought, if I could get to the altar. Then I would have won. I focused so single-mindedly on that goal, I never considered what I would really be "winning" or if I really wanted it. I just didn't want to admit that I was beat.

One of the best things I've learned from playing poker is not to throw good money after bad. You have to learn to stop thinking of the bets you've already tossed into the pot as an investment—as yours. No matter how many chips you've thrown in—or how many years you've spent with someone—it's gone now, and before you bet once more you have to consider what your hand is worth at that very moment. Is it still the best? Or have things changed? You can't win a hand simply by throwing more money at it, or make a relationship succeed just by accumulating time. As hard as it is to admit when you've thrown so much of yourself into a situation, you've got to face the simple fact that sometimes there's no way left to win. And when you know you're beat, the only move that makes sense is to fold and get out. It's not a matter of pride—it's a matter of knowing when you don't have any outs left and saving yourself needless loss.

It was a tough lay-down, walking away from my ex-fiancé. The allure of a royal straight flush (or a picture-perfect wedding) is strong—and I wanted to believe that he would eventually take a risk and go all-in on me, with me. It took a while, but in the end I looked at the board and let the cards speak. And when I did see the cards for what they really were, and not what I wished them to be, I saw that he would always lack the heart I needed to match my own.

YOU HAVE TO PLAY TO WIN

You could certainly enjoy watching poker or hearing about your friends' dates, but you're not going to get any action that way. Returning to the singles scene, the first thing I realized was that you had to be in a pot to win it, so I signed up for an online personals site. I told all my friends that they could set me up on dates: I was ready to play the dating game.

A lot of my friends were (and are) aghast at the idea of Internet dating. "What if someone I know sees it?" they say. "Isn't it kind of desperate?" they question. What's desperate is sitting around, endlessly checking your e-mail to see if the guy you sort of like maybe wrote back to you on a Friday night instead of going out with friends. Desperate is trying to appear like you don't need help meeting men when you do.

Dating is a numbers game, just like poker. Of every ten guys who answered my online personal, perhaps two were worth replying to. Of those roughly one in three were worth going out with once, and out of those, one in ten led to a second date. It seemed like fair enough odds to me, especially since the only investment I had to put in was time.

You can't expect that every reply or every hand will be a winner, but the more hands you play, the better your chances are of finding something good. And while you can't win 'em all, sometimes it sure is fun to play a lot of hands, even if at the end of the evening all you've ended up with is a story to tell and a few free drinks.

YOU'VE GOT TO BE WILLING TO TAKE RISKS

Of course I know that you have to take risks in life, but it wasn't until I spent night after night playing too conservatively, folding hand after hand, that I saw how not playing was just a slower way to lose.

I found that I could now look at the "risks" I sometimes feared in dating in terms of more realistic odds instead of blowing every decision out of proportion. For instance, asking a guy out. What was the real loss to me if I asked out Sir Crushalot and he said no? I would have to deal with the disappointment, but I'd get over it. If he was in my social circle, there'd be the awkwardness. I could put it on a scale—how likely, I would think, is it that he'll go batshit nuts at a party we're at? Longshot. Thousand to 1. Two to 1 it'd be cool. Even a "no" had the positive return of cutting off the "what if?" string of thoughts in my head, freeing it for more fruitful purposes. Or at least more fruitful pursuits. And what were the possible payoffs? He'd say yes. I might get some nookie. Awesome. I'll do that one.

Just like in poker, you can play a lot of hands, as long as you know you can walk away from them. And because you know there's always another man to e-mail, it's easy to let go of situations that aren't very promising. I no longer felt obligated to keep seeing someone just so I'd have a date on national holidays. And when I did start seeing a guy for more than a few dates and I saw he wasn't a fit, I was able to cut off things early and save us both time and possible heartache.

After all, unless you're having a damn good time, there's no reason to keep playing a hand just to play. Which reminds me . . .

YOU CAN LEAVE THE TABLE AT ANY TIME

I've only walked out on one date in my life, and I wouldn't have done it had I not played poker—even though I was clearly out on the bizarro freak date with the leader of the freak army. Pre-poker me would have convinced myself that it was only polite to wait until dinner was over, that another half-hour of hearing about every taxicab-confessions-like date he'd been on or tales of his "wild kid in the city" days wasn't really so bad. That I wasn't praying that no one I knew would enter the restaurant and see me with this military-jumpsuit-wearing, cologne-soaked wacka-doo. Old Toby would have grinned and bore it. Because it was the polite, kind thing to do.

But here's what poker-playing Toby did. Dinner had just arrived on the table as Sargent Freako continued on with his tale of teenage arson fun. I wish I were joking. As he rattled on, I looked at the food and I thought, *There is no way this dinner is worth one more minute of this. The odds of this situation improving over the next half-hour are zero. The chance is strong that this date will somehow,* though it seemed impossible at the time, *get worse*. I didn't owe this guy anything. There was no way I would ever see or talk to him again. I was tired. I thought, *I'd rather be watching TV*. And I didn't even have cable.

It hit me: my best move was to fold. No fancy dinner was worth this. I stood up, made my excuse, and walked away from a guy who I'm sure thought I was a total bitch. But what did I care what he thought of me? As soon as I practically burst out the door, I knew I had made the absolutely right move in listening to my gut and acting on it. I thought it was the best decision I had made all month.

GETTING PAST LOSING STREAKS

Just as in poker, one must admit that everyone, including yourself, has flaws, tells, bad habits that lead to losses, you can do the same with your love life. After going on the worst date of my life, I had to question the decisions I was making in my love life. As David Mamet wrote in "The Things Poker Teaches" (from *Read 'Em and Weep: A Bedside Poker Companion*, ed. by John Stravinsky, Harper-Collins, 2004), "Poker reveals to the frank observer something else of import—it will teach him about his own nature. Many bad players do not improve because they cannot bear self-knowledge. The bad player will not deign to determine what he thinks by watching what he does. . . . It is painful to observe this sort of thing about oneself. Many times we'd rather suffer on than fix it."

I didn't want to lose money at poker, and I didn't want to suffer through dating. Walking away from Seargent Freako was a good start, but I also looked at the factors that led to the date with him.

Internet dating was incredibly time consuming, so I had gotten lazy about evaluating a guy before I met him, and I realized that I had stopped expecting to meet someone I'd really click with this way. After four months of after-work drinks, coffee-shop afternoon meetings, and dinners where I more often than not had to feign interest in the conversation through the entire evening, I expected to be dealt a losing hand each night. I had switched from my A game to maybe a C game. I had lost confidence in the game—and just as I would if the same happened at the poker table, I realized it was time to get away and take a break from dating.

KNOW WHAT TO THROW AWAY AND KNOW WHAT TO KEEP

As I took myself out of the dating game, I decided it was time to think about what I wanted. I knew the things about my ex I didn't want, but if I couldn't identify the ideal hand, how would I know how to look for it?

Looking at the patterns of my life, I could see trends in the way I conducted my personal life, the things I was attracted to—and the things that led to some of my more disastrous relationships, first and foremost the ex-fiancé. The combination of having a competitive nature and stubborn streak led me to choose many of the men I became involved with because they were a challenge, because I wanted to win a guy's heart where all others had failed. Never been in love? Great! Never talk to your ex-girlfriends because it's always a bitter breakup? Where do I sign up? Not sure if you really love me? I'll make you love me! I'll become whatever it is you love. I'll make this hand fit and never fold.

Clearly, this was as losing a strategy in life as it is in Texas hold'em. You can't make the cards come to fit your fancy, no matter how hard you try, no matter how much you want the cards to fall in your favor. I saw that now—and I was done with it. I didn't want my next relationship to start with a struggle, with bluffing and check-raising and any underhanded technique I could use to try and stack a marked deck to my advantage. I just wanted to fit.

Beyond that, I wanted someone who felt he'd been dealt a lucky hand in meeting me. I was tired of men who were always hedging their bets, carefully doling out whatever love they thought they could afford. I wanted someone who is capable of making the grand gesture, of putting it all out there and making the leap of faith that any marriage requires. It's a scary decision to make, but if you look at it through the lens of poker, you know that it's the truth: you can't win it all without risking it all. It takes heart—that intangible mix of courage, faith, and desire—but one thing I already knew about myself is that love was a greater ambition than a gold bracelet, and I would gamble everything on it again, sooner or later.

THE RIGHT HAND AT THE RIGHT TIME

As luck would have it, it turned out to be sooner. In life as in poker, timing is everything. I wasn't looking for love, but spending the time just working on my own game and figuring out the kind of man I'd be willing to bet on in the future made me ready for it. So when lady luck shined on me and I found myself with someone who thought I was the stone cold nuts and would risk everything, all his heart on me, it didn't seem like a risk at all to push in all my chips and meet his bet. It felt like the right thing to do—that I had found the heart that matched with mine, a hand I could play until the end.

CHICKS WITH CHIPS: TIPS, TRICKS, AND GIRL TALK WITH TWO PROS

Women's all right. Only place in the world you can
beat one and not get thrown in jail is at the poker table.

—AMARILLO SLIM

n 2004, three women won the coveted gold bracelets at open events at the World Series of Poker—the largest number yet. Kathy Liebert conquered the limit hold'em shootout, Cyndy Violette triumphed in seven-card stud hi-lo 8-or-better, and Annie Duke reigned supreme in the Omaha 8-or-better event. They raised the total number of women winners (not counting those who won the women-only event) to ten. I was fortunate enough to get to chat with Cyndy and Annie, and pick the brains of two women who have played poker for years and excelled at the game.

ANNIE DUKE: CARD SHARPSHOOTER

In the first tournaments Annie Duke played in, not only did she knock her own brother, two-time World Series winner and two-time World Poker Tour champion Howard Lederer, out of the main event of the WSOP, she won over $70,000. Soon after that she moved her family to Las Vegas and began playing professionally.

After winning her World Series gold bracelet in May 2004, Annie Duke claimed her place at the top of the list of all-time money winners in the WSOP. She also placed tenth in the 2000 WSOP main event. Of women players, only Barbara Enright has placed higher in the main event—but Barbara wasn't nine months pregnant when she claimed her fifth place win. Annie is a dedicated mother of four children. Annie's the type who'd rather lose the "woman" qualifier and just be known as one of the best poker players alive, period. James McManus, author of *Positively Fifth Street*, compared her to Old West pioneer Annie Oakley, "the brand of gunslinger who only wants to draw to the baddest hombres walking her streets." Annie has played for a decade in high-stakes games almost exclusively against men. In fact, Annie stays out of all-women events not only because, she says, there's too much perfume, but also because she doesn't see the point. She explains, "poker is one of the only sports where a woman can compete on totally equal footing with a man, so I don't understand why there's a ladies-only tournament."

My kind of woman.

Toby Leah Bochan: Have you seen the attitude toward women at the table change over the years you've been playing?

Annie Duke: Well, I started playing in Montana. And Montana, as you can imagine, being the Wild West, was a much more male chauvinist sort of environment than even Las Vegas. That's not to say that I didn't come across a lot of male chauvinists when I did play in Las Vegas, but a little bit less just because I think that what happens generally, as you get more pros in the game, you get more people treating you as an opponent as opposed to as a woman. That's not to say that even at the highest levels there isn't some male chauvinism, but in order to succeed at the highest levels of the game, you really do have to treat people as they come and not allow your emotions to get in the way. But I was playing with a bunch of ranchers.

TLB: So were you the only woman at the table?

AD: I was basically the only woman who played in the game regularly. And I did have some people who treated me very well, who became very good friends, but I had a lot of people who really were very nasty to me. I got called a lot of bad names.

Not only was I woman, but I was also in my mid-twenties. And I was playing with mostly older men, ranchers, people on disability. I came in there and was my giggly self, and was taking their money. And when people were nasty to me I was nasty right back, which I'm sure they didn't like.

It was generally the people that I was taking money from who were not treating me well and didn't particularly like the fact that a girl, particularly a young girl, was coming in and basically fleecing them.

In Las Vegas, as I started playing 10/20 and 20/40, I did come across a lot of the same stuff. I remember one person who was hitting on me at the table and I was just kind of ignoring him and he ended up telling me that I was a frigid bitch.

In Vegas you're just more likely to come across women at the table [than in Montana]—people are just more used to it, but they still have the hitting-on-you reaction. I remember playing 3/600 one night and having a guy throwing my bets back to me after every hand—so I obviously tried to be in a lot of pots with him. At the end of the night, he leaned over as if to say something to me and stuck his tongue in my ear.

And I've been offered money, too—I got offered $35,000 for one night, which I was told was a "starter package." I got offered $2 million to marry somebody. And I said, "I'm already married," and he said, "so am I."

There are definitely people who disliked me because I'm a woman. I mean, I'm not going to name names but there were some top pros who definitely did not play very well against me, because they were clearly just male chauvinists.

TLB: I read an article on your Web site called "God Bless Men" in which you outline some of the strategies women can use against those types of players. So clearly it's something you've learned to take advantage of.

AD: That's the thing—it's not men in particular—there's an appropriate strategy against any opponent, because nobody plays perfect poker, even the best in the world. Everybody has weaknesses to their game; everybody has strengths to their game. It's just a matter of identifying how to leverage whatever it is—the errors that that person is making. And in the case of that male chauvinist, that's what I grew up playing against. Basically I never bluffed, because I got paid off every hand that I played.

TLB: That strategy isn't so different from how you'd play somebody going on some crazy tilt and playing every hand, right?

AD: Although people tilt in different ways. You have to be really careful when you use the word "tilt" because sometimes people are tilting in a way that is less obvious, where they're actually folding too often. Because they feel they're going to lose every hand. When somebody's tilting in that way, you're supposed to be bluffing that person a lot.

TLB: Is Omaha 8-or-better your favorite game or just the one you've had the most visible success with?

AD: I'm not sure that it's necessarily my *favorite* game, but the split games are definitely my *best* games. I'm really enjoying no-limit hold'em right now because—and this is going to sound kind of funny because I've been playing so long—but I've been doing a tremendous amount of work on my game over the last year. I actually sort of went into the second World Poker Tour Season just resigned to saying, I'm not necessarily going to do particularly well during the season because I really want to make some huge changes to my game.

And I've done that, and now have really been getting deep in no-limit and doing really well and have made a lot of money at it recently. I've always been a very good no-limit live player, but there are big adjustments you have to make in tournaments, and I don't think I was necessarily making the adjustments properly. I did a lot of work on it and that makes anything really fun. So I've been really enjoying no limit lately because I've just been making so many big strides and changes in my game.

But the split games are definitely my best games, and it also helps that in general the games that people play the worst are the split games, so if you're somebody who has a pretty deep understanding of those games—there's just a lot of money to be made in them.

TLB: In the past you've mainly played in live games and not in tournaments, so is that going to switch now?

AD: I've been playing in a lot of tournaments this year. In fact, I moved up to Portland because I didn't want to raise my kids in Las Vegas, so I've basically switched to playing exclusively in tournaments in the last year. And it's been a very profitable switch. I mean, not that I wasn't making a lot of money at live games, but it hasn't really affected my income to switch.

TLB: Speaking of tournaments, you were almost full-term with Lucy during the 2000 WSOP, where you finished tenth—can you talk a little about how it was to play?

AD: I *was* full term—I was only two weeks away [from my due date]. I had to go pee a lot. I was definitely really tired. And so I had to overcome my tiredness and obviously I was just uncomfortable and it's really hard to focus through a whole tournament when you can't even sit very well—by that time the baby was hanging pretty low. And I was huge—I was like 180 pounds. So it was a challenge just in terms of concentration and being able to stick out a tournament that at that point was four days long.

TLB: Do you think Lucy will be the one who plays poker of all your children? Do you expect to encourage, discourage, or let your kids make their own decisions about playing poker?

AD: Well, we'll see. My oldest daughter hasn't shown any interest—and I played a lot of poker while I was pregnant with her. I actually came in fifth in the championship event of the Hall of Fame in 1995, when I was seven and a half months pregnant with her.

We don't actually play cards at home. I don't really own any cards, because you know, it's what I do for a living. I don't think lawyers play lawyer with their kids. But if my kids express interest in wanting to learn the game, I'll definitely teach them. I'm not going to push them to be card players. I want them to do what they want to do.

My parents were teachers and I sort of went that way for a while, and found out it wasn't for me and obviously ended up doing something very different. I just sort of feel like you want to encourage kids to go their own way and fulfill what their potential is and likes and dislikes that they have.

TLB: On your Web site it says right at the top, "Professional Poker Player and Mom," so obviously being a mom is very important to you. Do you prioritize being a mother over being a poker player?

AD: Definitely. That's why I moved to Portland. I've skipped championship events because they happen to fall on a Christmas pageant show that I wanted to go to. The first year that the Bellagio ran a championship event in December, it fell on the same day as my son's Christmas show at school and so I just didn't enter the championship event. Another time, there was a huge game going on in Las Vegas that I skipped because it was my daughter's birthday. It cost me about $500,000.

TLB: Do you think being a mother has changed your game or vice versa—that being a poker player has affected how you are as a mom?

AD: Oh yes, definitely. I think they feed on each other. Poker is a game of tremendous patience and emotional control and emotional steadiness. I definitely bring that into my parenting.

There's a really important life lesson that you learn from poker, which is that nothing is ever that bad—and it will get better. The fact of being a poker player—particularly if you're playing tournaments—is that most days when you walk into work, you walk out a loser. That's just the way it is. You learn that bad things happening aren't the end of the world. It's not a big deal because you'll just come back and try again the next day and eventually you'll have success and at the end of the year you'll make money.

So you really do learn a little bit of a Pollyanna-ish attitude. You learn that there's a lot of things that are out of your control—you can't help if someone hits a 4.5 to 1 shot to you, and allowing yourself to get emotionally unhinged by that stuff is incredibly unproductive. You should just move on. I've definitely brought that into my parenting. I'm not a parent who gets freaked out when my kid has a fever. I'm not a parent who gets freaked out when the kids are fighting. I'm very sort of, "everything will be fine, let's all sit down and talk about it." And my kids are not very high-strung because of that. I have a very relaxed family because I've learned to be very relaxed. I've learned to get rid of that sort of high-strung attitude about what happens to you in life from poker.

At the same time, being a parent has really reinforced that. It's a very synergistic relationship because the fact is that whatever happens to you at the poker table, when you come home, and your kids are there, you know what's really important. And you know that the bad thing that happened to you that day is not particularly important because you can't come home to your kids and be emotionally unhinged and screaming at them and freaking out because, basically, you had a bad day at the office.

You know there are important things in life and there are nonimportant things in life. Taking a bad beat is just not a particularly important event in the scope of things. And I think that actually gives me an advantage over someone who might be a single guy. Because their whole life is poker, they don't have other stuff necessarily to balance it out, and they're going to get consumed by bad streaks. They're going to get consumed by good streaks as well, where their life might get a little out of control, when things are going really well. So my being a parent keeps me very grounded; it keeps everything in perspective.

TLB: Has your psychology background helped you at all? To read people, for instance?

AD: No, but the statistics side helped—understanding probability theory helped. To have a good understanding of the math is important.

TLB: Do you think the math is essential? Or can you just memorize the most basic odds and get away with it?

AD: There are close decisions that come up where you really do have to calculate the pot odds. But I think that as long as you know that with two to come, a flush draw's about a 2-1 dog, a straight draw's about a 3-1 dog. As long as you know those basics, you'll probably be okay in most games.

TLB: In terms of table image, does it bother you that a woman who plays right at the table gets called a bitch while men get to be "studs" or whatever?

AD: Of course it bothers me. People who know me in person know that I'm not a bitch but when I'm sitting at the table, I'm aggressive and I'm competitive and I'm extremely intense. As I should be. In a man, that's admired, like, "What a great competitor!" But in a woman, people are like, "Oh my god, what a fucking bitch." And you know what? I can't help that, so if you want to make a judgment about me when you've never sat down and had a conversation with me or met me in person, I can't really help that you want to do that. But obviously it hurts my feelings. But then people meet me in person and they're like, "Oh I totally was wrong about you."

There's not much I can do—I'm in a man's world. I'm in a world where in order to succeed you have to display a lot of masculine qualities. Whenever women display a lot of masculine qualities they're called bitches. I kind of compare it to the boardroom in the late seventies. There's a reason why those shoulder pads that were like, seven feet long and made you look like a football player became really popular.

Now, luckily, I don't have to wear those big shoulder pads—nobody's hiring or firing me based on what I look like. I'm allowed to just enter, so I can at least dress the way that I want to dress, which tends to be comfortable.

TLB: You do always look very comfortable, taking off your shoes, and I love watching you play because of it. But do you ever consider dressing more sexy or differently to use that to your advantage?

AD: No, because when I go into work I know I'm going to be there for ten, twelve hours. I'm not putting on a friggin' slip dress and high heels. Now when I go out to a club with my friends you can see me in 4-inch heels, in 5-inch heels and sexy tops—then I dress like a woman because I'm going out. But there's no way I'm going to go in to play in something that's going to be uncomfortable for the ten hours that I have to sit there. It's amazing to me when anybody says anything to me about it. "Oh, she only ever wears T-shirts and jeans when she's playing." It's like, have you looked at the guys? At least my clothes are clean. And it might be a T-shirt, but it's a designer T-shirt and I'm wearing high-end jeans. People are wearing sweatsuits!

NO SHRINKING VIOLETTE: CYNDY VIOLETTE

Cyndy Violette grew up in Las Vegas—her father was an entertainer who owned restaurants and who also gambled on sports. He always encouraged his daughter to play, and he watched proudly at the rail as she won her gold bracelet in the 2004 seven-card hi-lo World Series of Poker tournament. After eighteen years of playing poker and many other final table finishes, she exclaimed, "I did it, I finally did it," before calling her own daughter to tell her the happy news that mom finally took first place.

Violette has lived near Atlantic City since the early '90s, and can be found playing at the Trump Taj Mahal in high-stakes games every weekend. Among her fans there is the casino's owner, Donald Trump. When I spotted her there one weekend a few months after her WSOP victory, this fan had to congratulate her. Friendly and welcoming from the moment I shook her hand, she took out some time to talk shop with me about her experiences at the table and her hopes for the future.

TLB: Have you seen people's attitudes toward women players change over the decade (or more) that you've been playing?

CV: Well, when I first started playing poker, there weren't very many women playing at all. But I never really felt like I wasn't wanted or like they felt funny with me sitting at the table or anything. I always kind of just blended right in, and I don't want to say "one of the guys," because I was still a girl, but . . .

TLB: But you never felt or were made uncomfortable?

CV: Maybe once in a while. You come across some guy who thinks women belong in the home and in the kitchen and they don't feel comfortable playing with a woman.

One time in California, this guy was totally crazy. He couldn't stand me at the table. He was making remarks to me constantly. Real jerk guy, but you know you find one in every crowd somewhere along the line. But for the most part, I've been treated very well at the table and got along with everybody.

TLB: So you haven't really noticed any change.

CV: Only thing I would say is there are a lot more women playing poker now. A lot more women are feeling more comfortable. Before they felt like maybe it was a man's game and they didn't feel comfortable. But now, obviously, the more it becomes popular and more women are being seen playing, more women are playing, there are more ladies tournaments now, and it's evolved so much. Everybody's playing—women are part of everybody.

TLB: You started as a dealer in Vegas. Do you think that part of your being comfortable was that you've already been on the other side of the table?

CV: Yeah, it could be. I grew up in Las Vegas. I was always around gambling. My father gambled.

TLB: Was he also a poker player?

CV: No. Didn't play poker. He said my grandfather was a very avid poker player, though.

TLB: So you're the only one in the family that plays.

CV: Well actually, my sister started playing, too. She got involved. She wasn't very good, though. She was way too social. She was married, had four kids. So, for her it was such a social outlet. She didn't have the killer instinct. If she got friendly with the person next to her, there was no way she was going to raise them or anything. She was just too nice. She didn't have what it takes to be a professional player, but she loved to play. She passed away a few years ago. She played a lot when she was sick, too. She had cancer. So it was a very good outlet for her. It's a good way to connect with people and you're doing something at the same time, you know, and you have a common bond.

TLB: How did being a poker player affect your relationships? I know you were married at one point and you didn't play poker for two years.

CV: Right.

TLB: That wasn't what you expected when you got married.

CV: No, that was one of the things he loved about me when he met me. "Oh, you're a gambler!" He called me a "gambler." I wasn't a gambler. I was a professional poker player. *He* was a gambler. He loved the fact that I played poker. We got married very quickly, within weeks. I was married and I moved to Washington State. He kind of swept me off my feet. It was a quick romance and the next thing I know, I'm in Washington and now all of a sudden he became controlling and almost jealous of the fact that I played poker and didn't want me around other men. It was just a weird thing. But now I'm already moved to Washington. I got rid of my house, I got rid of everything I owned in Vegas, and I'm there and I tried to make the best of it, which . . . I mean, we went in and out of a lot of different issues and it was probably one of the best things that's happened to me because it did take me away from Vegas and poker for a couple of years and I saw what the rest of the world was like, you know—without gambling, without poker. That's what really made me look within, taking that time off. Realizing what I wanted in life. And I realized how much I love the lifestyle of being a poker player and I loved what I did. So that was a good break for me. And that helped me and I learned about a lot of different things.

TLB: How does your lifestyle help you at the table? I know you're a vegetarian and are into meditation.

CV: For me, when I prepare before I go play—like, when I do a meditation and I work out, I always do good. Always do better. But if there's something going on in my life, it always comes out on the table. If I'm having a bad day, something's going on in my life, or there's something on my mind, and I go play poker, I have a bad day. It's all connected. Whatever you do in your life in a way reflects on the table when you play poker.

TLB: I've noticed there's the typical attitude of poker players being . . . there's still a reputation for drinking and drugs, but I feel like the women aren't really falling for that.

CV: Poker has evolved so much. The image of poker is totally different. The reason why it was like that then is because that's what was going on then in the Old West. People were drinking in bars and that's where they would play poker. Now it's not like that. I don't see that as an image of a poker player, though. But it's part of the whole subculture. Different percentages of people that play poker are going to be into that and a different percentage might be into something else. It's just the way it is.

TLB: Playing as a woman player, do you find you can ever use being a woman to your advantage against the men?

CV: I don't do it intentionally, but sometimes it happens. It works two ways. One: sometimes you get free cards or they don't want to play hard against you. Or, they [do the] total opposite and they want to beat you so bad for whatever reason, their ego gets involved and they don't want to lose to you, so they might overplay a hand or try to chase you even more. So it takes them off their game one way or another. Not against professionals, but against some players that aren't . . . emotionally balanced. It triggers their male issues—or female issues or something.

To the people you play poker with all the time, they don't see you as anything. You're just a player. The gender doesn't come into the equation at all. People that don't play all the time, you can definitely trigger them.

TLB: You only work weekends. Why did you choose to only to spend time playing poker then?

CV: In Atlantic City, the high-limit games are only on the weekends. During tournament time, like today there's a game I'm playing in, but . . . like in California, there are high-limit cash games every single day, which is great. But it's also kind of nice to know that you only have to think about it on weekends. You know you're getting ready for the weekend. You don't let anything else distract you. It's much easier to get in the zone when you know you're only going to play Friday, Saturday, and Sunday. During the week, you can relax and get massages and do whatever you gotta do and spend time with your friends and family and do other things and not even think about poker—"Is there a good game? What am I missing out on?"—any of that. I like it actually, just playing weekends.

TLB: In terms of relationships, would you be more likely or less likely to date another poker player?

CV: Mainly, I've pretty much just gone out with poker players. It's just because the way you're around poker so much, that's where you meet people. Really, I don't want to anymore. I want to stay holistic. I really want to meet somebody that's more into the same things I'm into—that's the problem I keep running into. They're not into the things I really enjoy doing outside of poker, right.

TLB: You have that one thing in common, but then . . .

CV: Yeah, there's nothing else. I really want a guy that's vegetarian. I love going to vegetarian restaurants. And I love cooking and having friends over and going to retreats and working on yourself. I love doing all that stuff. I want my partner to also enjoy it. I want him to be on the same path.

TLB: Have you ever had any trouble because you've at the same table as someone you were dating?

CV: Actually, when I'm going out with somebody, we never, ever played at the same table against each other.

TLB: When you meet exes again at the table, do you know tells that they have that you wouldn't otherwise?

CV: I do have some inside information because we talked about poker. But, not really.

TLB: Can you talk a little about what it is was like to win the WSOP bracelet this year?

CV: Winning was a dream come true. Something I really wanted to do this year. I've never really had that desire before this year—I mean, I always wanted to win but I never focused on it like I did this year. And I did a lot of visualizations around it and meditations and to see it happen after doing all these visualizations I'd done was amazing. That was almost the coolest part of it. It was like I created it.

TLB: That's amazing. This wasn't the first final table you've been at?

CV: No, but I'd come close and I've had a block—like an actual block within me like I was blocking off success from myself for some reason. So to break through that—one of the tapes I was listening to was called "Clearing Blocks"—it was really a personal challenge to myself to win this tournament. It was great.

TLB: You didn't have that winning feeling going into other tournaments?

CV: No. I never put a lot of energy into it before. Now that poker's getting so big it's really much more motivating to putting energy into playing tournaments instead of cash games.

TLB: Seven-card stud is your best game—have you noticed it getting edged out by hold'em?

CV: I play seven-card stud day in and day out. At the Taj, stud is still popular—there's a lot of good games every weekend—but hold'em is really popular. But in my opinion, seven-card stud is such a better game than hold'em. There's a lot more skill involved. It's just a much more skillful game. Much more to it. Hold'em has a lot more luck, so much more guessing for me.

I mean, if you get unlucky in seven-card stud, there's another hand to play—it'll even out. But if you get unlucky in no-limit hold'em, then you're out. You don't have the chance to get that back—you're out. I still play it and I'm planning to get better at no-limit hold'em. I'm going to start playing on the Internet—I haven't had time to right now, but I'm going to get better at it. I used to play it all the time. When I first started playing that was what I used to play—that's what was popular back then, and it died out. I was pretty good at it. Because I play so much seven-card stud and I've only played no-limit hold'em in the big tournaments, I haven't really gotten back into that no-limit hold'em mode yet.

TLB: How does your daughter feel about poker?

CV: My daughter has really no interest in playing poker. I've tried to get her to play—but it's just not her. To her, she doesn't know any different, so—since she's been a baby I've been playing poker. Actually, I learned poker when I was pregnant with her.

TLB: Did you learn just by playing or did you read books to help?

CV: I really just learned by playing. I really didn't read any books.

TLB: Are you a math person?

CV: Nope. Not at all. That's another thing that scares people off from poker—"oh, I don't know math." I don't either! I don't know math at all. A lot of it's feel.

TLB: Do you calculate pot odds and stuff like that?

CV: Yeah, but I don't know them in a mathematical way— I know them just from knowing. I have a feel for it, that's all. It's not true at all that you have to know a lot of math. As a matter of fact, I think the best players play more from their heart and their soul when they play, versus their head. They're more in touch with their intuition; they're more in touch with the game.

People that play from their heads and are so analytical— there's no flow to their game. They never really are in touch with what what's going on. And for me, that's my style—I try to tune in to the game, get in flow, try to connect with what's going on in the game, where people are at.

One day this guy might be on the top of his game, and another day he comes in and he might have had a bad day that day, and you need to know that. That's the first thing I do when I get in the game—I see where they're at: are they winning, are they losing, do they look like they're tired. You can talk to them and find out where their head is at. Everybody plays different depending on what's going on in their life. There's no one way to play a person, and even the same person plays different on different days, so you have to be able to gauge that.

TLB: Do you think that'll be an advantage that women will have over men at the table?

CV: Probably, because most men are more analytical and women are more in touch with feelings, so definitely that is where a woman could have an advantage.

TLB: If you had one wish about poker, one thing you wish was different about the poker scene, what would it be?

CV: That seven-card stud would be on TV more. A lot more. I'd like it to become more mainstream. Maybe after everybody gets tired of hold'em that'll happen. The other thing I'd like to see is that the real World Series champion should play all games. It should be a five-game tournament—you play, and every half-hour you switch games, hold'em, stud, every game should be played. And *that* should be the world champion—all those games should be played. Maybe the final table could be no-limit hold'em or something, but to get there you have to play every game. That would be my wish, that it was more of a mixed game thing to win the world title. It would be more based on real skill.

❧ EXTRA CREDIT ❧

BADASS CHEAT SHEETS

WHETHER YOU'RE POSTING THESE CHEAT SHEETS FOR ALL THE vixens at your girl's poker night, or you're simply stashing them in your pocket for your own sly reference, these tearouts will make the whole thing more fun. And ultimately . . . that's the point.

THE RANKS OF HANDS

From the best hand to the worst:

2 ♥ 3 ♥ 4 ♥ 5 ♥ 6 ♥ **Straight Flush**

Five cards, of the same suit, in order.

10 ♠ 10 ♥ 10 ♦ 10 ♣ 5 ♠ **Four of a Kind**

Four of the same card.

9 ♠ 9 ♥ 9 ♣ 7 ♥ 7 ♦ **Full House**

Three of a kind plus a pair.

2 ♣ 7 ♣ 8 ♣ 10 ♣ K ♣ **Flush**

If your cards are smartly dressed, all in the same suit, but a little out of order, you've got a flush.

8 ♦ 9 ♥ 10 ♣ J ♠ Q ♦ **Straight**

Five cards in numerical order, but not of the same suit.

J ♣ J ♦ J ♠ 7 ♦ 3 ♠ **Three of a Kind**

Three's good company.

6 ♠ 6 ♣ 2 ♦ 2 ♠ A ♥ **Two Pair**

It's kind of like a double date.

8 ♣ 8 ♦ J ♠ 5 ♥ 2 ♣ **Pair**

Sometimes a couple just wants privacy.

A ♥ Q ♦ 10 ♠ 7 ♠ 4 ♣ **High Card**

If there's no pair, no nothing, just a jumbled mess of numbers and suits, players pit their highest card against one another. Just hope yours is an ace.

QUICK AND DIRTY GUIDE TO PLAYING TEXAS HOLD'EM

If you just want to get right to playing the Cadillac of poker, here's how to do it like a pro in no time.

1. The two players to the left of the dealer put out *blind bets*—meaning they each put in a set amount before any cards are dealt.

2. Every player is dealt two cards, face down, called the hole/pocket cards.

3. The action falls on the player to the left of the blinds. She can either call the bet, raise it, or fold. Betting continues around the table.

4. After the betting is complete, the dealer "burns" a card (deals one card face down on the table), and then deals three cards face up in the center of the table, which is referred to as the "board." The first three cards are called "the flop." These cards are "community cards," meaning everyone can (and will) use them in combination with their own hole cards to make the best hand.

5. From the flop on, betting begins with the player to the dealer's left, who can check or bet.

6. The dealer again "burns" a card, and then deals a fourth card face up on the board. This is called "fourth street," or "the turn card."

7. There is another round of betting.

8. The dealer "burns and turns" another card. The final card is called "fifth street," or "the river."

9. A final round of betting occurs. The remaining players show their cards and the person who can make the best five-card hand by combining their pocket cards with the cards on the board wins. In some rare cases, the five cards making up the board will actually be the best hand, in which case everyone left in the hand divides up the pot.

20 TABLE TERMS

Here's the vital vocab you need to know to not get beat up on the poker playground.

Action—Used a few ways: if the game's stalled, someone might ask, "Where's the action?"—they're asking whose turn it is to bet. If it's your turn, they'll tell you, "The action's on you." Or it's used to describe the betting itself. "The game has a lot of action," means there's a lot of betting and money changing hands.

Bad beat—When a really good hand is beaten by an even better hand. Especially used in hold'em when a hand that is favored to win is beat because the other, weaker hand got a lucky card on the river.

Bump—To raise. "Bump it to fifty" means raise the total bet to $50. Also see "kick it."

Burn—In hold'em and Omaha, the dealer discards the top card, face down, before turning up the three-card flop. The discarded card is the "burn card." The dealer burns a card before dealing fourth and fifth streets as well.

Button—A round marker used to show who the dealer is in a hand. Also called a "buck."

Family pot—When everyone (or almost everyone) at the table stays in a hand, you've got a happy family pot.

Heads up—When a hand or game comes down to just two players. Also called "head to head."

Kick it—Raise the bet. If you're raising a $10 bet by another $10, you'd say, "Kick it up to $20."

Limp—To bet the minimum or simply call. In hold'em, when the little blind simply meets the big blind bet as opposed to raising, the little blind is "limping in."

Muck—As a noun, a discarded hand, or the pile of discarded hands. As a verb, to fold your hand.

Nut—The best possible hand in games with community cards is called "the nuts." Also used with a particular hand, such as "the nut straight" or "the nut flush"—meaning not only do you have a flush, you've got the unbeatable flush.

Position—Where you sit in the order of betting during a hand of poker. The players who are first to act are said to be in early position, and the last ones to act are in late positions. Also used as a verb: if another player gets to act after you, she's got position on you.

Post—To put in a bet. Usually this refers to a forced bet, like a blind. If you had stepped away from the table for a bathroom break someone might "post" your blind for you.

Rake—A fee charged by the house to play. Also called "chop."

Riffle—To shuffle your chips.

Roll—To deal a card face up, as in "Roll the next card."

Stack—Your total chips on the table. If you've got fewer chips than most other players, you're "short stacked."

Toke—A tip, usually for the dealer. Comes from *token*, as in "a token of appreciation."

Tilt—When a player lets her emotions affect her play negatively.

Under the gun—The first player to act in a hand is said to be "under the gun."

CONCLUSION

THE WAY WE PLAY NOW: WOMEN AND POKER'S FUTURE

Women are meant to be loved and not play poker. My wife Helen Elizabeth thinks that a king is a ruler of a country and a queen his bedmate. A woman would have a better chance of putting a wildcat in a tobacco sack than she would of coming out to Vegas and beating me.

—AMARILLO SLIM

ood old Amarillo Slim, "Mr. Poker," one of the living legends of the game, can always be counted on for some colorful quotes to accompany the cards at the table. This rail-thin, straight-talking Texan epitomizes the Old West image of poker: just look at his Stetson, banded with the skin of a rattlesnake that bit him. Amarillo also maintains the belief that women can't play and once swore he would slit his throat if a woman ever won the main event of the World Series of Poker. While Barbara Enright broke the final table seal in 1995 and finished fifth, no one's forced him to make good on his promise. Yet.

Things are changing. While there's still those who believe that poker is a man's game, as the years have passed and poker's reputation has changed, so has the belief that women cannot be great players. Even many poker players, such as David Spanier, have changed their tune. Spanier once said that "the *machismo* of poker is significant. It is the characteristic of the game. Not that women are excluded, but the virtues of successful poker, which have colored the game since its earliest days, are the swashbuckling male qualities of courage, aggression, and bluff." This stalwart believer in men's superior ability years later admitted, "Women are no longer considered as accessories to be brought to the poker table, but as equals at the game."

Equals is a good start. But there's no reason to stop there. James McManus, author of *Positively Fifth Street* and fifth-place finisher in the 2000 WSOP, wrote that women have the ability to be better than men in poker, and echoes a popular sentiment that women have "superior ability to read emotions and psychology." The founder of the World Poker Tour, Steve Lipscomb, is a big fan of female poker players and has said, "The fact is, women can play better than men." He believes that if more women entered his tournaments, "the poker world would be changed forever." The recent major wins of the women at the WSOP and the high ratings of the premiere of the World Poker Tour "Ladies Night Out" on the Travel Channel prove that change is already well underway. The show broke new records—its 5 million viewers making it (at the time) the most-watched poker game ever. On Bravo's Celebrity Poker, there's always at least one lady among the celebrities around the felt and they're not only holding their own—they're winning, again and again.

Women, while still outnumbered, are no longer a shock at the poker table. And more and more women are playing—one survey finding that women players in their twenties and thirties now outnumber male players in their forties and fifties. Web sites like the Women's Poker Club have emerged to help and encourage ladies to play, and gaming Web sites geared to women are starting to pop up. In Vegas, the Rio has created a new 21,000-square-foot entertainment complex just for women where they can experience "The Ultimate Girls' Night Out," and while its more a place to party than play poker, it is the first of its kind. And it's a bright, flashy sign that women are being taken more seriously as a part of the casino scene—not just as dates or wives along for their partner's gambling trip, but as players themselves.

And why not? There's nothing to stop us from sitting down and playing. If you've got the money, honey, there's always an open seat. Personally, I'm hoping to find an open seat with my name on it for this year's World Series, and I would love to be the first woman winner of the main event. I've got a long way to go and a lot to learn before I get there, and I have the feeling that before I do, another one of the women will win that coveted title and bracelet. After all, when a woman sets her sights on getting something that glitters, she'll do whatever it takes to get her hands on it. It won't be long before one of the fairer sex closes the clasp on the gold bracelet and with it, closes the lid on the doubts and debates on whether women can equal men at the table. The cards will speak the inevitable answer—we most certainly can.

RECOMMENDED READING/BIBLIOGRAPHY

This book just scratches the surface of all there is to learn about poker. And with the hundreds of books in print about poker, this list just touches on the many manuals and accounts that have been written. The following books and resources were all incredibly helpful to me both as I first started studying the intricacies of the game and as I wrote this book. While I probably learned as much from the memoirs and journalistic accounts of the players as I did from the nitty-gritty manuals, I've split the list into two sections, so you can find just what you want to continue your poker education.

MEMOIRS AND REPORTING

Alvarez, A. *The Biggest Game in Town*. Boston: Houghton Mifflin, 1983.

Bellin, Andy. *Poker Nation: A High-Stakes, Low-Life Adventure into the Heart of a Gambling Country*. New York: HarperCollins, 2002.

Holden, Anthony. *Big Deal: A Year as a Professional Poker Player*. Toronto: McClelland & Stewart, 1990.

Lederer, Katy. *Poker Face: A Girlhood Among Gamblers*. New York: Crown Publishing, 2003.

Konik, Michael, *Telling Lies and Getting Paid*: *Gambling Stories*. Guilford, Conn.: The Lyons Press, 2002.

McManus, James. *Positively Fifth Street*. New York: Farrar, Straus, and Giroux, 2003.

HOW-TO'S AND STRATEGY

Bruson, Doyle. *Super System: A Course in Power Poker*. Las Vegas: B & G Publishing, 1978.

Cloutier, T. J. and Tom McEvoy. *Championship No-Limit & Pot Limit Hold 'Em*. New York: Cardoza Publishing, 1997.

Nestor, Basil. *The Smarter Bet Guide to Poker*. New York: Sterling Publishing, 2003.

Sklansky, David. *The Theory of Poker*. Las Vegas: Two Plus Two Publishing, 1992.

Steiner, Peter O. *Thursday Night Poker*. New York: Random House, 1996.

ACKNOWLEDGMENTS

Without my wonderful editor and dear friend, Kate Epstein, this book would not have been possible—and not just because she came up with the idea. I hope I never again have to write a book in as short a time as I wrote this one, but without Kate's suggestions, support, and enthusiasm, I wouldn't have made it. Thanks also to my lawyer, Nina Graybill, for guiding me through everything, and my boss, Michael Daecher, for letting me take so many days off.

I owe a huge debt to all the members of the Thursday night game for so warmly allowing me to join in the game and the immense fun, but especially Jesse Angelo, Martin Auster, Fipp Avlon, Simon Clark, Jake Kreilkamp, Alex LeVine, Felix Salmon, and Kelly Thomson, who have all helped me out in countless ways beyond schooling me at the poker table. A special thanks to Greg Clayman, who first brought me into the warm folds of the Thursday night game, and went above and beyond what any friend could rationally expect in terms of help. Thanks also to Dave Landau for showing me around the New York City poker scene and Andy Bellin for his advice and help.

I'm very grateful for all my friends who helped me keep my sanity through their advice or just by buying me a beer, especially Jennie Auster, Laura Krinock, Joe Turner Lin, Marilyn Suzanne Miller, Jeremy Olshan, Vanessa Reisen, Lydia West, and Ginny Wiehardt.

Thanks to all the ladies who attended my poker classes, but especially my friend Sigrid Benedetti, who allowed chicks with chips to overrun her restaurant, Hope & Union, and supplied many a takeout bag of delicious treats to keep this writer going. I would like to give a special shout-out to her bacon scallion rolls, which are almost as wonderful as she is.

The best big blind hand I was ever dealt was being paired up with the incredible Amanda Clayman in the dorms my freshman year of college. Without her friendship, love, and support not only over the past two months, but throughout the past twelve years of my life, there is no doubt I would be neither the person nor the writer I am.

Finally, my love and thanks to Matt Law, who managed to make me laugh every day during one of the most stressful periods of my life, and for believing I was a good bet right from the beginning. Matt, you're the absolute nuts.

INDEX

ABOUT THE AUTHOR

TOBY LEAH BOCHAN was hooked on poker at the tender age of seven when her progressive New York City parents let her join in their home game. After spending four years in Michigan and three in Austin working on her other love, writing, she returned to New York City with an MFA. You can find her Thursday nights playing with the guys; Sundays playing with the girls; and when that's not enough, in poker rooms in Manhattan and Atlantic City. Her writing has appeared in *Threepenny Review, Other Voices, Post Road,* and *Red River Review,* where it was nominated for a Pushcart Prize.